There Are No Utes In Utah

HISTORY of the UINTA VALLEY SHOSHONE TRIBE of the UTAH NATION

By DORA VAN, TRESSA JORDAN, & JOHN TORRES

ISBN 978-1-66785-309-3 (Print)

ISBN 978-1-66785-310-9 (eBook)

Dedicated to the Uinta Valley Shoshone people
past and present. Whose remarkable survival
defies those who intended to do us harm.

To our ancestors, thank you for your sacrifices, strength,
and wisdom. Your guidance has saved us from genocide.

Thank you to the people (Newe) and our families,
your belief in us has kept us going through the difficult task of
writing this book. The anguish of our ancestors could be felt
throughout our research and at times it was difficult to proceed.

To our future generations we will teach you our true history, and
with this knowledge, you will be able to keep the wolves away.

Spanish warning to Mexico's Mesoamerica (1500s):

"That if you don't submit, we shall take your wives and your children and make them slaves ... and we shall take away your goods and shall do you all the harm and damage we can."

Table of Contents

Preface

This book is a compilation of archaeological research, newspaper articles, tribal records, BIA and Interior Department documents, Smithsonian, and other important records. The spelling of places and names within the documents varies, depending on the time-period and the individual writing. This is a corrective history of who the Native Americans were that inhabited the Utah Territory. While current usage often favors the term "Native Americans" this book will use the term "Indians", to reflect the common nineteenth-century usage. Early settlers didn't find out who the indigenous people were or from what tribes they belonged. They twisted the truth and referred to them erroneously as unknown Indians (Utes). The Utahs and Shoshone are the original inhabitants of the Utah Territory. The Utahs have never had a ratified treaty with the United States Government and still hold title to all their original lands. This is the early history of the Uinta Valley Shoshone Tribe of the Utah Nation. We have always been called Utahs and the State is named after us. The State of Utah tends to rewrite history and publish a false story. For the truth always refer to the federal documents.

Introduction

The history of the Uinta Valley Shoshone people is put into a written form to preserve and protect it from being lost to those Americans who lie, hide, and distort the history of Native Americans to feed their own private agenda of greed, self-enrichment, genocide, theft, and destruction of people and property in the perceived name of righteousness. The Uinta Valley Shoshone Tribe is made up of many bands of 'Yutas' or 'Utahs' (the spelling of the word depends on the user of the word but in any case, it means "Shoshone") who fled the Salt Lake Valley after the Mormons moved into the Great Basin in 1847, when the landed area was still held in the ownership of the Republic of Mexico. The Yuta-Shoshone Culture secured the Basin and the bands branched out in a fanlike pattern over the landed area into southeastern California, southeastern Oregon, southern Idaho, the western half of Wyoming, the Uinta Basin in northeastern Utah, and the western half of Colorado to the crest of the Rocky Mountain's west side, occupying nearly all the Great Basin by the time the Europeans began to arrive.

The U'-in-tats, Seuv'-a-rits, San'-pits, Ko'-sun-ats, Tim-pa-na'-gats, Tim-pai'-a-vats, and Pi-ka-kwa'-na-rats bands of Yuta-Shoshone Indians have been in continuous existence in the Great Basin since the 1100's. It became Utah Territory in 1850 after Mexico ceded the territory to the United States in 1848. The Utah Shoshone roamed the lands from present day California to Northern New Mexico. They encountered the Spanish Explorers in the 1700's and were documented in their reports as Yuta's. They befriended early trappers such as Jim Bridger and would meet at Fort Bridger in the early1800's to trade. Their existence was documented in the Latter-Day Saints records beginning in 1849 and after Brigham Young became Governor and Indian Agent of the Territory in 1850. The tribe's existence continued to be documented every year after that in the Commissioner of Indian Affairs Reports to the Secretary of the Interior. In 1861 The President of the United States Government, Abraham Lincoln, created an Executive Order Reservation in the Uinta Basin specifically for the various bands of Yuta or Utah Shoshone who collectively became known as the "Uinta Band". The reservation was called the Uinta Valley Indian Reservation and was ratified on May 5, 1864 (13 Stat. 63). In 1865 the Indian Agent O. H. Irish conducted treaty negotiations with the various Yuta bands at Spanish Fork, Utah Territory, however, this treaty was never ratified by Congress. Once the United States Indian Affairs Department began keeping Indian Census on the Uinta Valley Reservation in 1885, the names of our Uinta ancestors became a federal record, proving again our people existed. These Uinta Indian Census Rolls were completed again in 1888, 1891, 1894, 1895, 1913, 1929 and 1944.

The Secretary of the Interior continued to keep federal rolls on our people and in 1954 he created the Affiliated Ute Citizens of Utah (Yuta) and provided a Federal Constitution, in order too, maintain the United States Governments federal membership and kept our community alive. We gather-together in family groups throughout the year to collect and preserve the various foods on our lands, we hunt, fish, and keep to the annual traditions that feed our families. We practice our traditional religion, utilize our sweat lodges and dance, drum and sing to our ancestors. Our people were intentionally scattered by the Latter-Day Saints (Mormons) and some were forced to leave after 1954, but those people all knew where home was and after nearly 70-years of exile, the descendants are returning to the extended families that remained, to finally recover the reservation land granted by the 1861 executive order to the Uinta Valley Yuta-Shoshone Tribe, to re-take their tribal identity and begin again – as always.

The Native inhabitants of the early Americas did not view the land (mother earth) upon which they traveled and lived, or the land's natural gifts that sustained them, as possessions. They were gifts of life from the creator. They did, however, respect territorial boundaries between the bands and family clans for the preservation of their people that was, on the most part, respected by the various other bands, living in proximity in the same area. These various tribes of natives were not under any one single leadership in the same way as the Europeans who were under the rule or management of one political body or person of one nature or another, who, under that rule or management, were commissioned to journey to the Americas from foreign countries as explorers, immigrants and ultimately so-called conquers. The arrival of the Spanish in the lands that came to be known as the Americas was an invasion, not a discovery. The pattern was established at the beginning. Once he arrived on Hispaniola (Dominican Republic and Haiti), Columbus immediately began gathering Arawaks to take back to Spain to sell in the slave markets. He had his brother do a census to determine how many male inhabitants over 14 could provide tribute (over a million). He found the source of gold used in an ornament given to him by one of the local Native Chiefs, and immediately impressed Arawak men to work the mines. If they didn't produce the requisite amount, a hand or a foot was cut off. The brutality of the Spaniards, was so extreme one of the accompanying priests called it a "fierce and unnatural cruelty." The early Spanish explorers were not the only cruel invaders that would be a detriment to the indigenous people of North America. Throughout Native American history, their lives and culture have not been valued by those trespassing on their lands.

Colonial – "The wonderful and unsearchable Providence of GOD in the whole Affair of driving out the Natives and planting Colonies of Europeans, and Churches of Christians, in the Place of Heathenism and Barbarity. "Thinning of Indians" by disease to the "hand of God, eminently seen."[1]

United States – President Andrew Jackson stated in 1833, "That those tribes cannot exist surrounded by our settlements and in continual contact with our citizens is certain. They have neither the intelligence, the industry, the moral habits, nor the desire of improvement, which are essential to any favorable change in their condition. Established, in the midst, of another and a superior race, and without appreciating the causes of their inferiority or seeking to control them, they must necessarily yield to the force of circumstances and ere long disappear."[2]

---

1 Rev. John Callender, An Historical Discourse on the Civil and Religious Affairs of the Colony of Rhode-Island and Providence Plantations in New-England in America, 1739, excerpts.

2 President Andrew Jackson, in his fifth annual message, December 3, 1833

General Sheridan stated, "The only good Indians I ever saw were dead."[3]

Church of Jesus Christ of Latter-Day Saints (Mormons) – "There is a curse on these aborigines of our country who roam the plains and are so wild that you cannot tame them. They are of the house of Israel; they once had the Gospel delivered to them, they had oracles of truth; Jesus came and administered to them after the resurrection, and they received and delighted in the Gospel until the fourth generation, then they turned away and become so wicked that God cursed them with his dark and benighted and loathsome condition; and they want to sit on the ground in the dirt, and to live by hunting, and they cannot be civilized. And right upon this, I will say to our government if they could hear me, "You need never to fight the Indians, but if you want to get rid of them try to civilize them." How many were here when we came? At the warm Springs, at this little grove where they would pitch their tents, we found perhaps three hundred Indians; but I do not suppose that there are three of that band left alive now. There was another band a little south, another north, another further east; but I do not suppose there is one in ten, perhaps not one in a hundred, now alive of those who were here when we came. Did we kill them? No, we fed them. They would say, "We want just as fine flour as you have." To Walker, the chief, whom all California and New Mexico dreaded, I said, "It will just as sure kill as the world, if you live as we live." Said he, "I want as good as Brigham, I want to eat as he does." Said I, "Eat then, but it will kill you." I told the same to Arapeen, Walker's brother; but they must eat and drink as the whites did, and I do not suppose that one in a hundred of those bands are alive. We brought their children into our families and nursed and did everything for them it was possible to do for human beings but die they would. Do not fight them

---

3 General Philip Henry Sheridan, 1869

but treat them kindly. There will then be no stain on the Government, and it will get rid of them much quicker than by fighting them. They have got to be civilized, and there will be a remnant of them saved.[4] "The day of the Lamanites (Indians) is nigh. For years they have been growing delightsome, and they are now becoming white and delightsome, as they were promised. In this picture of the twenty Lamanite missionaries, fifteen of the twenty were as light as Anglos; five were darker but equally delightsome. The children in the home placement program in Utah are often lighter than their brothers and sisters in the hogans on the reservation. At one meeting a father and mother and their sixteen-year-old daughter were present, the little member girl-sixteen sitting between the dark father and mother, and it was evident she was several shades lighter than her parents on the same reservation, in the same Hogan, subject to the same sun and wind and weather. There was the doctor in a Utah city who for two years had had an Indian boy in his home who stated that he was some shades lighter than the younger brother just coming into the program from the reservation. These young members of the Church are changing to whiteness and delightsomeness. One white elder jokingly said that he and his companion were donating blood regularly to the hospital in the hope that the process might be accelerated.[5]

---

4 Brigham Young – Discourse given in the new Tabernacle on April 9, 1871.

5 Church of Jesus Christ of Latter-Day Saints, Prophet Spencer W. Kimball, General Conference, Oct. 1960.

The Early History
of the
Uinta Valley Shoshone Tribe
of the Utah Nation

CHAPTER 1:

Fremont-Yuta-Shoshone Culture

From the crest of the Rocky Mountains in Colorado, west to the crest of the Timpanogos Mountains (called Wasatch Mountains on the east side of the Salt Lake Valley in the Great Basin) is the land of the "Uinta Band of Yuta-Shoshone Indians. The Uinta River Valley Basin Reservation lies at the crest of the Uinta Mountains on the north and runs south along the Colorado border to the Book Cliffs just above I-70. It consists of approximately 5.5 million acres and has been the exclusive ownership of the Uinta Valley Shoshone Tribe of Yuta-Shoshone Indians since 1861. Archaeologists have uncovered the remnants of the ancient archeological culture they call the Fremont which includes the ancestral Yuta-Shoshone culture throughout the Uinta Basin, central Utah, and into eastern Nevada and western Colorado. Although it is on the eastern fringe of the area once occupied by a people known to archaeologists as Fremont (an archaeological label, not a homogenous "people"), Colorado is nevertheless important in the Fremont story, since clues to their origins and disappearance are found there. The presence of Fremont farmers had a profound influence on the indigenous hunting and gathering people of western Colorado, eastern Utah and across the Great Basin of the West. From an archaeological perspective, the Great Basin Late Prehistoric/Protohistoric era is divided into two distinct periods: Saratoga Springs (Fremont Culture), (A.D. 500-1200) and the Yuta-Shoshonean period (A.D. 1200 to European contact to the present day). This narrative will attempt to trace the origin and migration of these ancient Mesoamerican Cultures and connect them to the Fremont and the historic Yuta-Shoshone Indians of the Great Basin and with the modern-day Shoshone whose ancestors dominated the Great Basin with the horse in Western Utah and most of the western United States west of the Rocky Mountains in the 17th and 18th Centuries.

Prehistory and History Summarized

Unlike native tribes before and after them, the Fremont in the Great Basin were primarily sedentary. They built villages of pit houses with adobe structures to store food. They collected wild foods and hunted game, but also cultivated corn, beans, and squash using irrigation techniques. The presence of obsidian (volcanic glass), turquoise, and shells show that the Fremont traded with distant villages. The Fremont differed in several ways from their more famous contemporaries in the 11th and 14th centuries, the Ancestral Puebloan peoples who built Mesa Verde and Chaco Canyon. Four distinct artifacts set them apart: a unique "one rod and bundle" basketry construction, moccasins constructed from the hock of a deer or sheep leg, the classic trapezoidal shaped figures found as clay figurines and in local Rock Art, and the unique materials used to make their gray, coiled pottery. Settlements were of surprising complexity. Instead of a scatter of pit homes and mud-walled food storage structures the villages consisted of an organized cluster of buildings built according to a specific plan and aligned to a single compass direction. In the center, a larger mud-walled structure shows intriguing alignments with sunrise on the winter and summer solstices. All traces of Fremont culture disappear from the archeological record between 1300 and 1500 C.E., several climate changes are thought to be the cause. But where did they come from? Paleo-Indians settled in all the un-glaciated corners of both North and South America. They followed shoreline migration routes or inland routes between glaciers. The three different periods of glaciation affected not only coastline locations but climate, environment, habitat, vegetation, and animal life. Western Hemisphere migration routes from 10,000 B.C. have been suggested by archaeological sites along these corridors. Mexico City was settled around this same period. The absence of sites in California (except on islands) has been explained by the fact that during the glacial age the coastline was three hundred miles out to sea. This suggests the variety and extensiveness of migration routes and why migration stories are central to Native American cosmologies (the natural order of the universe). According to oral traditions, travelers went in all directions, not simply north to south.[6]

Settlement in the Sandia Mountains of New Mexico was found dating back to 25,000 B.C. The Clovis-era human was far more numerous than the Sandia and Clovis stone points have been found in every state of the continental United States; 28,000 B.C. is the earliest known date for Mesoamerican inhabitants on California's coastline. California's early settlers left hearth charcoal on Santa Rosa Island, off the coast, attesting to inhabitants who lived along

---

6 The Fremont Complex: A Behavioral Perspective, David B. Madsen and Steven R. Simms, Journal of World Prehistory, Vol.12, No. 3 (September 1998).

the California coast at least 30,000 years ago. They followed several different migration routes along the California Coast and inland in Central and South America. The floor of the Bering Sea (a permanent body of water between Alaska and Russia), emerged as dry land during the late Pleistocene glacial advances, around 28,000 to 10,000 B.C. Asian hunters followed big game herds migrating from Siberia into Alaska along this route and began settlement in western Alaska about 27,000 B.C. (See "The Bering Land Bridge or Berengia").

The final Ice Age occurred between 10,000 – 7000 B.C. the glaciers began to melt. The melting marked the end of large-scale migrations from Siberia. Over the next 3000 years climate changed dramatically, with natural shifts in vegetation and habitat for big game species. Many mammals gradually became extinct and native inhabitants whose livelihood was based on hunting big game like the woolly mammoths, had to shift their settlement patterns as well. Paleontologists believe that as societies tried to replicate the growing of wild plants, they became more sedentary and their economies more diversified. 9000 B.C. saw the beginning of agriculture in Mexico. Inhabitants of south-central Mexico in the Valley of Tehuacán began to experiment with a wild grass called teosinte. They kept seeds and began to germinate new strains of the grass, which eventually evolved into what is considered ancestral to maize, or corn. Settlement sites throughout North America suggest a migration route down the California coast to southern California, across Arizona, New Mexico, and Texas; then heading northwards to Illinois and the Great Lakes, and across to the Atlantic coast. Settlement sites of this period in North America show a great variety of tools, trade goods, and burial relics.

In Columbia River sites in Oregon archaeologists discovered diverse tools related to salmon fishing; in California many settlements sites were located around San Diego and Lake Mohave; in Michigan not far from Detroit archaeologists found tools such as scrapers and projectile points; in Utah archaeologists discovered sites with remains of wood, leather, fur, and basketry. In the Great Basin area, where early residents (Fremont Indians) lived in caves or rock shelters, archaeologists found basketry, grinding stones, sandals, the atlatl (a club or throwing stick), small stone points, digging sticks, smoking pipes, seashell ornaments, deer-hoof rattles, medicine bags, and bird-bone whistles. Such artifacts reflected complex trade networks as well as a diverse economic life. Teotihuacán, Mexico rose to prominence while hordes of barbarians were swarming Europe, causing what is called the European Dark Ages. Teotihuacán, Mexico was the first great civilization to appear in central Mexico where Mexico City is today. It began in the first century B.C. (CA. 1 - 2000 years ago) when the big population centers in the Mexico basin, Cuicuilco and Tlapacoya, were having internal difficulties. Eventually Teotihuacán's rulers realized they had over centralized the city and executed a planned repopulation of the Mexico Valley to better manage agricultural production and exploitation of natural resources. The geographical area dominated by Teotihuacán in the basin of Mexico was probably not more than 10,000 square miles, about the size of Sicily. Its influence was economic, religious, and cultural, based on trade that extended as far south as Honduras and as far north as the Mississippi Valley in today's United States.

The list of what is known about Teotihuacán is short: It lasted over 700 years; for most of the time everyone lived in one city organized on a grid plan – a pattern which did not exist before or after Teotihuacán in Mexico; its pyramids were among the biggest in the Americas and were built in the beginning of the city's history, the first century; It was laid out according to a newly devised astronomical orientation; Permanent multifamily apartment compounds were built to house the population for the last 500 years of the city. The walls of many were painted with murals; Its principal deity was a goddess; The rulers did not glorify themselves in art; and, sometime around A.D. 750-800 it came to a cataclysmic end. The destruction of Teotihuacán was deliberate, systematic, and ritual. The city was sacked, possibly by the Chichimec, invaders from the north. Palaces were burned. Temples were reduced to rubble. Its destruction was so complete, it seemed that the intent of the destruction was for the city never to rise again. It was never rebuilt, but a small population lived on the ruins for another century. The Aztecs who occupied it centuries later viewed the earlier civilization with great respect. Prior to Teotihuacán's ultimate destruction, its ruling elite fled north to the provincial city of Tula, where its leaders and artisans re-created the wonders of Teotihuacán. Tula became known as the capital of the Toltecs and flourished between A.D. 900 and 1100, repeating much of the culture and theocracy of the earlier city. It is believed that it was the Toltec inhabitants of Tula who traveled to outlying colonies and then by sea or land along the Gulf Coast into the Mississippi Valley and north up the Pacific Coast of North America.

People from Mesoamerica (a term used to identify the advanced societies of central and southern Mexico and the Yucatán) migrated north along several different routes and took up permanent residence in the Four Corners area of the Colorado Plateau (Utah, Colorado, Central Arizona, and the mountains of New Mexico) They would become known as three distinct peoples, the Hohokam, the Mogollon, and the Anasazi. The Mesoamericans, over centuries of experimentation developed a sophisticated horticulture with other seeds and roots. They carried with them the knowledge and tradition of their ancestors who eventually produced maize (corn), beans, legumes, chili peppers, avocados, gourds, squash, cocoa, and, most important, cotton, which would serve as an important trade good. The colonists from Mexico migrated along the Gulf Coast and throughout the river system of the Mississippi watershed. They left thousands of temple mounds in the form of truncated pyramids and a system of terraced farmlands like those found in Mexico. They built with earth rather than stone and grew maize, beans, and squash as well as a variety of other agricultural products. The migration from Tula in Mexico, the new center of Mesoamerican civilization, formed the cultural and historical bridge between the ancient Teotihuacán and the modern Aztecs who still ruled in Mexico at the time of Cortés (1519).

Southern California was settled in 5500 B.C. by people from Mesoamerica referred to as the Encinitas Culture. Grinding stones and shell remains suggest an economy based on the sea and farming marine resources. In the San Diego area, the Encinitas tradition endured until 1000 B.C. Northern California settled around 4500 B.C. These first Californians built sturdy, semi-subterranean earth lodges. As the climate warmed, they shifted to lighter surface dwellings made of brush. The Encinitas migrations took them east to the Great Basin where they settled in the peripheral areas available around the Fremont who had arrived in the Great Basin sometime between 400 and 800 B.C. The Encinitas people later divided into linguistically distinct people, the Yuta, and Shoshone.

The Archaic Indians of California lived during the period from about 8,000 B.C. to 1,000 B.C., they lived in permanent villages, buried their dead in mounds, and made shell ornaments and beads which were widely used in trade. They also made bowls, pipes, and baskets and they were the ancient ancestors of the major indigenous cultures of the Yokuts, Miwok, Maidu, Wintun, and Ohlone natives of today.[7]

The indigenous peoples of Mesoamerica in the Americas shaped their societies around agriculture and highly inventive horticultural techniques, which were often supplemented by fishing and hunting. The laborious processes involved in gathering and germinating roots and seeds, and finding ways to store foods, formed a crucial part of the knowledge and technologies of these early cultures. Corn would eventually change world agriculture. Today, corn is half of America's agricultural output. Arizona and New Mexico horticulture began with the cultivation of maize, beans, and squash. Farming techniques were like those found in the Valley of Mexico. These Mesoamericans are believed to be the ancient ancestors of the later Hohokam and Mogollon peoples and the modern-day Pueblo peoples of Arizona and New Mexico.

The Anasazi who settled in the drainage area of the Little Colorado and San Juan River about A.D. 100 became known as Western Anasazi; those who settled on the Rio Grande and Chaco River were known as Eastern Anasazi.

The Mountain area of New Mexico was settled by the Mogollon. To the southwest along the Gila and Salt Rivers were the Hohokam Indians who began farming in the Gila and Salt Valleys of what is now Arizona around 300 B.C. following a similar agricultural practice found in Mexico along the Salt River in Arizona and began an irrigation farming system that is the basis of modern-day Phoenix. From the years 1000 to 1300 Anasazi communities flourished in New Mexico, southern Colorado, and northern Arizona and the Four Corners area. At Chaco Canyon, New Mexico, the Anasazi

---

7 Uinta Fremont – Ashley National Forest – History and Culture, https://www.fs.usda.gov

residents built, Pueblo Bonita, considered the highest expression of Native American architecture in North America. The Bureau of Land Management surveyed the Chaco Road system by aerial photography and identified over 500 miles of Anasazi roads that were straight, thirty feet wide, and excavated down to bedrock. It is believed that the roads were used to bring agricultural produce from the outlying areas. The Anasazi sites all had similar characteristics. They were centralized sites surrounded by large, cultivated fields and one-story houses of multiroom dwellings. They had highly specialized agricultural systems that included growing two crops a year of maize, beans, and cotton. They used irrigation canals and knew how to tap groundwater by digging wells. Because of cataclysmic volcanic eruptions in Alaska that caused significant climate changes there and in northern Canada in A.D. 825 and 1000, Athabascans began moving south along separate migration routes. One group migrated along the coastline into what is now the Washington and Vancouver area. The other group followed the inland migration route into the Great Basin and still others down into what is now Arizona and New Mexico, where they settled areas adjacent to the Anasazi and later divided into two linguistically distinct people, the Navajo and the Apache who become separate and distinct groups by the fifteenth century.

The population of North American Indians was believed to have reached its height between A.D. 1200 and 1300. Some estimates go as high as 110 million people in the Western Hemisphere during this time. In the 1300's the Mississippian sites began contracting and the large sites in the Southwest were abandoned. One theory for the decline is that an epidemic disease at this time spread throughout North America. But disease was not the only factor.

The Spaniards who arrived in the Caribbean and in Mexico in the next century brought with them disease, the medieval mind of Europe and a sense of economic purpose shaped by the gold and slave trades of Africa. Far from settling a virgin continent, Europeans moved into preexisting Indian villages and followed Indian trade route into new territories using Indian guides. What the natives did not realize until it was too late was that European Christianity made it impossible for the Europeans to view the Indians in a way that allowed a fair or equitable co-existence. They saw the natives (Indians) as savages, as a people without a culture, valuable only as a source of slave labor. The Spanish warned: "We ask and require you ... to acknowledge the Church and the high priest called the Pope as superior ruler of the whole world." That if they did not submit, "We shall take you and your wives and your children and shall make slaves of them and we shall take away your goods and shall do you all the harm and damage we can." And they did.

In order, to pay off the conquistadors without depleting the royal treasury, the Spanish Crown gave land grants along with the labor of the 'Indian vassals' who lived on the land. In return for a specified number of Indian laborers, the Spaniards were expected to protect and instruct them in Christianity. By the time the native leaders realized that they did not understand European think-ing and their only hope lay in war, it was too late. Some, like the Tlaxcala of Mexico, who allied themselves with Cortés and thought they could put the Spanish horses and guns into service against their greatest enemy, the city-state of Tenochtitlán, met the same fate as the Aztecs they helped to defeat. The 15th century experi-enced a massive invasion by Europeans beginning with Columbus's fourth and final voyage in which he was shipwrecked off the coast of Jamaica, But Spanish rulers knew they had found a New World and put in place the administrative apparatus to govern it. The capital of New Spain was at first in Havana, Cuba, then in Mexico City. In 1519 Hernando Cortés ignored the governor's orders to explore the mainland of Mexico and instead decided to conquer it. Scholars have reevaluated his victory in terms of the epidemic diseases that ravaged the city of Tenochtitlán. Disease is the ghost figure that accompanied the Europeans in all their contacts with Native peoples: Cortés in Mexico; De Soto in Florida, Georgia, Alabama, and Mississippi; Coronado in Arizona and New Mexico. Ninety percent of the population they encountered were believed to have been eliminated by epidemics of measles, chickenpox, and smallpox to which the natives had no immunities. In 16th century Mexico millions of people died. They were replaced by black slaves, shipped in chains from Africa to the European colonies and plantations in the New World. While the Spanish invaded from the south, dominating the Caribbean, the Gulf Coast, and the American Southwest as far as California, the French invaded from the north. By the end of the 1500's France was entrenched in what is now Canada, had mapped the entire Mississippi Valley, and established a few settlements on the Carolina coast. In 1588, after England and the Netherlands had defeated the Spanish Armada, they began to plan colonies on the Atlantic Coast in the areas of New England and New Amsterdam (New York). The destruction of the Armada marked the end of the Spanish ascendancy and the beginning of English domination in the New World. Every twenty years the Spanish had ripped open a larger tear in an ancient fabric. Native leaders were facing a new enemy, the true nature of which they had only begun to comprehend. The descendants of the great Mississippian cultures were virtually wiped out within the century, devastated by a combination of guns, epidemics, and slavery. But like the stories of all ancient cultures throughout the western United States of America their cultures live on in oral traditions, in recovered artwork, in place names and archaeological remains that tell their story to the world today.

Fremont Indians Throughout Central Utah

A chronology is a description of linear time, a chain of discrete events which must include developments such as plagues, migrations, religion, and climate which take place over centuries. "Mesoamerica" is a term applied to Mexico and the Pre-Columbian cultures that radiated out from Mexico. The American Southwest – Texas, New Mexico, Arizona, Southern California, Northern California, and the Great Basin (the largest such basin in the United States). Shaped like a bowl and surrounded by highlands; the Rocky Mountains standing to the east, the Sierra Nevada Mountain Range to the west, the Columbia Plateau to the north, and the Colorado Plateau to the south. The "Great Basin Culture" area, where numerous indigenous groups shared a similar lifestyle for centuries, includes all of Nevada and Utah, parts of Idaho, Oregon, Montana, and California south into the tip of Northern Mexico, were all lands settled by ancient Mesoamerica colonizers. The Fremont Culture was not restricted to the Great Basin, it spanned around the same time A.D. 800 as the Hohokam people who were farming thousands of acres of desert land in Arizona. Anasazi culture from Mexico established communities that flourished in New Mexico, southern Colorado, and northern Arizona from approximate years A.D. 1000 to 1300. Discovery and recognition of Fremont distinctiveness from these cultures was dismissed early on by anthropologists as being a peripheral sub-culture of Anasazi with whom they were more familiar. The Fremont settled in the Great Basin of Utah and Nevada about A.D. 400 to

1250 and even later in some districts and Fremont distinction was delayed because of its superficial resemblance to the Anasazi which has been determined to be a separate and distinct culture.

The Fremont people adopted farming into their subsistence patterns, they grew corn, beans, and squash, but their diet usually included a wide array of wild foods and wild game. A new culture developed from multiple roots as the change from purely foraging-based diet, it shifted to a dependence on cultivated foods. Interaction between migrants and locals led to new complex artifacts, behaviors, and beliefs. One important development, shared by the Fremont and their foraging neighbors, was the adoption of the bow and arrow, a significant change from the spear-like darts propelled by throwing sticks that had been the main weapon for thousands of years. The bow and arrow changed hunting strategies, and at the same time there was an increase in the diversity of wild foods that were collected and processed. Fremont area populations increased in the adjacent uplands (mountains) in response to these changes. The term "Fremont" describes people whose territory stretched from eastern Nevada to western Colorado, and from southern Utah north to southern Idaho and Wyoming. The Fremont people were highly mobile hunters and farmers who inhabited the Salt Lake Valley of the Great Basin and a wide radius of land throughout the Great Basin from around A.D. 200 to 1300 before disappearing. Their sites occur in a fifty-mile-wide swath along the Utah/Colorado border, from Grand Junction, Colorado north to the Wyoming border and west across the Great Basin. Nine-mile canyon located on the Uinta Valley Indian Reservation is approximately 40-miles long and is known for its exquisite rock art, created during the Fremont culture. Fremont roots go back about 2000 years; they disappeared about 500 years ago.

Uinta Fremont

From about A.D. 1 to 1600 a group of natives in northeastern Utah, including north of the Uinta Mountains and adjoining areas in northwestern Colorado relied extensively on maize horticulture as an economic strategy. Commonly referred to as the Uinta Fremont, this group shared the characteristics of the Fremont in other parts of the state of Utah. The Uinta Fremont started farming during a particularly favorable climatic period 2000 years ago when the local area was slightly warmer and wetter than other areas. Families generally lived in small, scattered farmsteads or rancherias during this period. The people had adopted the bow and arrow and horse in addition to two-handed manos and trough shaped metates. (Stones used for grinding seed, grain, and corn).

Archeologists speculate that after A.D. 500 the climate changed. There was more seasonal variation, and the weather was generally drier, with periods of drought. After generations of successful farming, the people struggled to maintain this lifestyle in the deteriorating conditions. The population may have shifted and coalesced onto better-watered drainages from the Uinta Mountains during this period. Between A.D. 500 to 1300 is the classic Fremont phase in this area. The population peaked around A.D. 900. Large village sites occurred on major tributaries like Dry Fork, Brush Creek, Uinta River and Simmerman Creek. Most habitations were pit houses, but a number of surface jacal, (a hut with a thatched roof and walls made of upright poles or sticks covered and chinked with mud or clay), structures could indicate a transition to another habitation structure later in the period. Granaries and storage structures are existing everywhere throughout the region and along the major tributaries, entire alcoves were devoted to storage. In several of these overhangs, considerable effort was used to create large storage units that were dug into bedrock or lined with clay and rock.

Rock art was an important trait of the Fremont. Some of the rock art seems to have been used to mark important dates as a solar calendar or almanac to ensure an adequate harvest at the extreme edge of maize agriculture; to commemorate significant events or individuals; or created for ritual reasons, such as to ensure a good hunt or record a dream or vision. Personal ornamentation was important to the Uinta Fremont. Their rock art shows elaborately decorated individuals. Many decorative bone and stone beads and pendants have been found in excavations. The Uinta Fremont made the typical split one-rod and bundle Fremont style basketry, but all the known burden baskets from this area have decorative elements, usually a zigzag, stairstep or lightning shaped design of colored fiber woven into the basket. The Uinta made a limestone tempered pottery that was usually made into globular two handled pots. Several pottery sherds from the periphery of the Uinta Basin suggest that temper or clay containing calcium carbonate, not just exclusively limestone, was purposely selected for ceramic making. Rose Spring projectile points, often of exquisite material and craftsmanship, were made during the Fremont era. The main agricultural centers in the Uinta Basin may have been abandoned by A.D. 1200 to 1300. However, peripheral groups that lived along Red Canyon and in Browns Park in the Uinta Mountains continued to persist until at least A.D. 1550. These groups relied on maize agriculture during the growing season and made logistical upland visits in the fall to collect chenopod (herbs) and hunt large mammals like deer and mountain sheep. This diverse economic strategy allowed these groups (Uinta-Ats) to persist much longer than the Fremont in the rest of the states.

When and How the Fremont and Shoshone Culture Developed We begin with the Saratoga Springs era (500-1200). The Proto Shoshone settled on the periphery of the Great Basin by at least 1050, sharing the region with the "Fremont" Culture, which anthropologists identified by their maize/corn cultivation, coiled basket-making, and pit house construction. It is believed that due either to environmental changes for which they were simply better adapted, or perhaps because of the Proto-Shoshone's more aggressive habits, the Shoshone were able to secure the Great Basin for themselves upon the exit of the Fremont people from the landscape. The Yuta and Shoshone Indians (settlers who migrated from California's Encinitas culture) lived around the periphery of the Great Basin and east to the foot of the Uinta Mountain Range in northeastern Utah around the end of the abandonment by the Fremont Indians about A.D. 1300. Archaeologists now think of the development of the Fremont Culture in the Uinta Basin as a process of interactions that occurred between people who were looking for good farmland in the highlands of the Uinta Mountains and the people who already lived there. The area was not completely abandoned; there is good evidence that some Fremont people were able to return to foraging by using the resources of higher terrain, where cooler temperature and more precipitation continued to make foraging viable. Other Fremont no doubt migrated elsewhere. A.D. 1637, in the lands of Utah and Colorado, the Spaniards of New Mexico sent slaving parties into Shoshone Country to raid villages and capture slaves to take back to Spaniard settlements in New Mexico. In the process, many of the kidnapped Shoshone escaped, taking with them Spanish horses. Their possession of horses subsequently made the Shoshone one of the most powerful Indian Nations of the Great Basin in the west. In time, use of the horse would spread throughout the Great Basin and change the culture of the Plains Indians. The Proto-Shoshone branched out in a fanlike pattern from the Great Basin of Utah into southern California, Southeastern Oregon, south Idaho, the western half of Wyoming, and the western half of Colorado, eventually to occupy nearly all the Great Basin and lands eastward to the Great Plains by the time the Europeans began to expand to the West and the Mormons began to arrive and settle in the Salt Lake Valley of the Great Basin in 1847.

The 1700's was a period of land cessions. The Native people of North America and Canada were primarily influenced by having to choose between alliances with France and England; and secondly by the variety of local and regional governmental entities taking their lands – by agreement, by treaties, by land cessions, and by theft. While the geopolitical struggle was between France and England, the local struggle was between Indian nations allied with either the French or the British. The French seemed primarily interested in trade, with widely dispersed trading posts and missions; while the English seemed land hungry, intent on settling the land with endless numbers of colonists. By the end of the 1700's the English colonies had become the United States of America and native people of both coasts had been decimated by war, removal, slavery, disease, economic deprivation, and missionary excesses.

The Shoshone-Speakers (Paiute and Goshute) and Yuta whose language and dialect was somewhat different from Shoshone or Snake dialects, were in possession of the Great Basin and surrounding territory by A.D. 1300. These Tribes protected the Archaic Lifeway that had remained characteristic of the entire Great Basin from the beginning – with foragers of the desert. There is no evidence of any archeological nature that the Fremont's "reverted" to the archaic practices, they farmed. The linguistic evidence is firm as to the time and direction of expansion of the Shoshone-Speakers although there is repeated evidence of dual use of camp locations by both cultures. Likely more toward the end of the Fremont era.

As the Numic-speaking Shoshone spread, their lands came to border a number of other sub-groups of the indigenous Shoshonean culture of the region including todays Washo (of California and Nevada), the Northern Paiute (of Nevada and southern Oregon), the Uinta Valley Yuta-Shoshone-Uinta-Ats (of central and eastern Utah and parts of western Colorado), the Southern Paiute (of southern Nevada, southern Utah, northern Arizona, and southeastern California), the Kawaiisu (of California's Mohave Desert), and Owens Valley Paiute (of Owens Valley, California and a portion of Nevada).

During the American Expansion, in 1800, the Shoshone also split into three distinct subdivisions as they fled the Salt Lake Valley and the Mormons: The Northern Shoshone (in southern Idaho; a territory shared with the Bannock), Eastern Shoshone (primarily in Wyoming, western Montana, and Uinta Valley in northeastern Utah), and Western Shoshone (based in eastern California, central and northeastern Nevada, Oregon, and northwestern Utah). According to Shoshone oral history, by the year 1500, the Shoshone with the use of the horse had crossed the Rocky Mountains and begun their expansion toward the Great Plains. By 1700, a group of Shoshone had migrated into the southern Great Plains, eventually developing their own identity as the Comanche, and migrated to Texas. The Taos Indians of New Mexico abandoned their pueblo in 1639 and traveled to Kansas with Spanish horses and introduced horses to the Kiowa, Comanche, Wichita, and other southern Plains Indians. The Siouan-speaking peoples of Minnesota migrated to the northern Great Plains and did not exist as a horse culture until the 17th century. Following an intertribal dispute, Dakota bands from Minnesota split from their allied tribes and began a series of migrations which took them as far west as the Rocky Mountains and south into the Great Plains. There they used the horse and adopted a buffalo-hunting culture. The Rocky Mountain bands became known to the Europeans as Assiniboine, the Great Plains bands as Dakota or Sioux. The Dakota and Assiniboine both spoke a Siouan language.

Conclusion

Genetic approaches to the past, hypothesize that one of the many Central Mexican empires, possibly the Toltecs or the Aztecs, or both spread the genetic DNA marker to the peripheral groups in which it is found today. Data does not fully support the Southern Origin Model of the Uto-Aztecan theory (Hill 2001) but rather support previous studies that indicate Mesoamerica populations had little maternal genetic influence on populations of the Southwest (Malhi et al. 2003; Smith et al. 2000). The Fremont Culture is separate and distinct from that of the Anasazi culture, the Hohokam, and the Mogollon cultures from Mesoamerica, who are believed to be the ancestors of the modern Pueblo peoples. The Yuta-Shoshonean culture developed during the same time and from the same origins (but not same groups) as the Fremont developed in the Great Basin around 400-1350 A.D. The Uinta Basin Fremont development was 650-950 A.D. The Uinta Valley Shoshone Indians living on the Uinta River Valley Reservation in northeastern Utah are today's descendants of these historic and ancient cultures.[8]

---

8 Anthropological Papers – Caldwell Village No. 84, By: J. Richard Ambler University of Utah December 1966.

CHAPTER 2:

Yuta-Shoshone

When you think about the ancient ancestors of Native Americans, view them as a family of brothers. The origins, culture and traditions are the same but the brothers each developed their own family, lifestyles and culture separate from each other. Influenced by family placement, location, habitat, environment, availability of water, food sources, shelter, opportunity, and leadership. All these conditions played an important role in the development and identity of each family characteristic including variations in language and dialects. Some families were affluent; others struggled with environmental conditions, others were aggressive and war-like, and yet others developed skills for industry and trade. Mastery of all these factors and more was for the welfare and survival of the family and its culture. Sometimes the brothers got along and sometimes they didn't, sometimes they became estranged from one another in ways that broke the bond of brotherhood and they forgot they were brothers … but the genetic connection has always been present even unto today's descendants.

The following is a general statement of Archaeological findings that suggest the Fremont Indians were one of many groups of Mesoamericans (a term applied to Mexico and the Pre-Columbian cultures) that radiated out from Mexico to inhabit the American Southwest – Texas, New Mexico, Arizona, and Southern California – were all part of Mesoamerica. Research holds that the Fremont in the Great Basin to the north of the southwest cultures, was a separate and distinct culture from the ancestors of the Hohokam, Mogollon, and Anasazi Cultures that had settled in the Four Corners area of the Southwest. By the year 300 B.C. these cultures had settled sites in the Southwest where they farmed and planted beans and corn, following a similar horticultural practice and irrigation process found in Mexico. Other groups of Mexico's Mesoamericans took different routes north along the coast to Southern California then split and spread in all directions by 100 B.C. California's Encinitas migrations took migrating groups to Northern California, Oregon, and lands due east into the Great Basin where the "Fremont" ultimately settled. The first Yuta-Shoshone (or Proto-Shoshone) groups of Mesoamericans settled on the periphery of the Great Basin by at least 1050 B.C., sharing the region with the "Fremont" that dominated the Great Basin of the West until their departure around 1300. The Proto-Shoshone entered the Great Basin but were confined to the peripheral areas and highland (mountains) available around the Basin and areas to the east of the Great Basin due to regional competition from the "Fremont" until they disappeared. The departure of the Fremont Indians freed the ancestors of the Yuta–Shoshone groups living on the periphery, to secure the Great Basin for themselves after which they dominated and branched out into the lands of the Great Basin that encompassed the whole of Utah and the greater portion of the West and expansion into areas of the Great Plains region of the United States. The

Yuta-Shoshone group known as Newe (pronounced nuh-wuh) which simply means "people", divided into family groups that, over time, evolved into linguistically distinct families developing variant features of dialect in the common Shoshonean language, specialized skills, personalized lifestyles, and traditions.

Having adapted to the most barren expanses of land in the Western Continental United States, the early Yuta-Shoshones formed small, isolated family groups of 6 to 8 people that were constantly on the move in search of seeds, roots, fish, birds, small game, and the occasional antelope or Mountain goat. The early Yuta-Shoshone timed their cross-country foraging based on the maturation of plants and abundance of game, returning year after year to the same locations for harvesting. Once divided regionally, the various Shoshonean groups became reliant on what was most locally abundant, and they self-identified according to their primary food source, thus becoming known as "Diggers," "Seed Eaters", "Rabbit Eaters," "Bird Eaters," "Fish Eaters," "Buffalo Eaters," etc. Equally diverse were their harvesting needs and locations.

To survive long winters in the Great Basin, seeds, fish, and other meats had to be dried and carefully stored. Food supplies were typically stored in caches in the ground, rockpiles, or caves. With the promise of spring, foraging became the group's top priority, they all set off in search of new grass, bulbs, and wild lettuce. After the immediate area was thoroughly harvested, they broke camp and moved to the next harvesting ground or to nearby lakes or swamps where they could harvest cattail, collect the eggs of ducks and other fowl, and use hand crafted bird decoys to lure waterfowl to nest so they could be snared or taken with bow and arrow. When spring began, the attention turned to hunting game, even though big game merely supplemented plants, fish, and fowl as food sources, it required special skills and equipment.

With the onset of summer, fish and game become less available, so the Yuta-Shoshone would focus on gathering again and wherever possible, they cultivated the soil. At this time of year, the Newe (people) traditionally left the dry desert floor for higher elevations, seeking hillside patches of bulbs and roots, gooseberries and bull berries, wild seeds and grains, wild onions, and garlic, most of which required considerable processing to be eaten and stored. For storage, grains had to be winnowed, ground, and prepared as cakes, while broad leafy plants like spinach had to be soaked to remove the bitterness and then dried. This practice continued until fall when they harvested pine nuts and conducted rabbit hunts. The Yuta-Shoshone also collected medicine plants such as wild rye, wintergreen, strawberries, bear root, water lilies, sunflower seeds, lupines, wild roses, iris, squaw berries etc., which were used to treat colds, sores, rheumatism, and other ailments. In times when food was especially abundant, it was common practice for families of several groups to gather and form a camp, where they would spend time interacting, singing, dancing, and storytelling.

The Yuta and Shoshone Tribes were inter-related and occupied a vast area of land in the high desert regions between the Sierra Nevada Mountains and both east and west of the Rocky Mountains in what is now the State of Colorado; territory that was at that time, claimed by the Republic of Mexico. The territory described had been home to these indigenous people of the Great Basin for thousands of years; (as far back as the Ancient Freemont Culture 400 A.D. to 1350 A.D., whose petroglyphs and artifacts are found all over in the Uinta Valley Basin). The Shoshone Territory included all the territory of what is now, the southern regions of Oregon and Idaho, eastern California through Nevada, Utah, Montana, and Colorado, Western Wyoming, and a portion of Northern Arizona.[9]

---

9 Anthropological Papers – A Study in Culture Contact and Culture Change the Whiterock Utes in Transition No. 15, By: Gottfried O. Long University of Utah Press February 1953.

CHAPTER 3:

Explorations of North America

Between 1100-1400 prior to and during the Spanish era of known expeditions, between 1400-1600, Spanish records do not indicate when or where but only that there were over 250 Secret Expeditions around the globe licensed by the King of Spain, they were specifically in search of sources of precious metals. The expedition records held in the Spanish National Archives, in Madrid, Spain suggest many of these secret expeditions took place in North America in the area west of the Rocky Mountains all the way to the Pacific Ocean.

By 1500 A.D. the Shoshone had acquired the horse and crossed the Rocky Mountains and begun their expansion toward the northwestern Plains. By 1700 a group of Shoshone had moved into the Southern Plains, eventually developing their own identity, lifestyle, dialect, and traditions as Comanche, and migrated to Texas.

In 1525, Spanish rule in Mexico and Central America was nearly complete, it took yet another year until 1526 for the Maya societies to be defeated before the Spanish could push further north in a new campaign of Spanish Northern Expansion.

In 1526, Spain began its northern expansion into the northern unexplored territory, which was to become New Spain. (North American west) The Spanish pushed quickly to seize as much land as possible in the northern expansion of the arid north; this was motivated to prevent the British or the French from encroaching onto the newly claimed territory of New Spain. The English and France had already claimed joint ownership of what is Washington, Oregon, Idaho, Wyoming, Northern Colorado, and lands north into Canada.

From 1535 to 1820, the Spanish claimed a political unit of Spanish territories referred to as the Viceroyalty of New Spain. These lands included present-day southwestern United States, Mexico, and Central America. The vast expanses north of New Spain, including present-day Utah, were explored in 1776 by Domínguez and Escalante, and accordingly claimed by the Spanish Empire. The Mexican War of Independence (1810-1821) resulted in the expulsion of the Spanish colonial government with the authorization of the Treaty of Córdoba. Consequently, Mexico gained independence as a constitutional monarchy and acquired the lands presently defined by the country of Mexico and the states of California, Nevada, Arizona, New Mexico, Texas, Colorado, and Utah.

Historic accounts written by Pedro de Castaneda, the chronicler of the Coronado expedition, suggest that Don Garcia Lopez de Cardenas may have entered southeastern Utah in 1540 in search of a large river reportedly lying northwest of Tusayan, the Hopi villages in northeastern Arizona. Additional accounts during the periods of the Cortez and Coronado expeditions mentioned the lands of Lake Copala and El Gran Teguayo located to the north-west of the pueblo villages of New Mexico and Arizona. Historians presume that these lands were probably in the vicinity of Utah Lake and Great Salt Lake.

By 1540, two Spanish Conquistadors Captain Garci-Lopez De Cardenas and Francisco Vasquez De Coronado led an expedition with 300 conquistadors and 1000 native slaves this expedition discovered the Grand Canyon, the expedition could not go any further. Cardenas returned to Santa Fe failing in his mission to map a route to the Pacific Ocean, however, it is believed Coronado continued north into modern day Utah and continued north in search of the fabled seven cities of gold that made up Quivira and Cibola.[10]

Coronado's expedition is unaccounted for until his return to Santa Fe the capitol of New Spain in 1542 with a story of his arrival in Kansas and his failure to locate the lost cities of gold. Coronado was then licensed by the King of Spain to take charge of colonizing New Spain, this a prestigious appointment lasted until his death in 1554. The Spanish never traveled north beyond the Uinta Mountains, and it is speculated that Coronado found the very rich ancient gold mines in the Uinta Mountains, which he reported to the King of Spain and was rewarded by his appointment.

In 1603, Martin De Aguilar's served on the Spanish frigate Tres Reyes Commanded by Sebastian Vizcaino whose job was charting the California Coast and Martin De Aguilar was to explore the lands inland on a route from Cove Blanco in New Albion to Lake Superior. The route taken by the expedition led them over the Sierra Nevada Mountains through the Great Basin and into the Uinta Mountains then over the Rocky Mountains on to Lake Superior. It is speculated that this expedition and the route it took resupplied the Spanish Garrison with food, horses, and conquistadors in the Uinta

---

10 Exploration of the American West – Meeting of Frontiers, https://www.loc.gov

Mountains. The records from the Spanish National Archives in Madrid, Spain do not show the expeditions arrival at Lake Superior, however, Martin De Aguilar passed away enroute to Acapulco later in 1603 while returning from the expedition, as noted in Sebastian Vizcaino's expedition diary.

The route that Martin De Aguilar's expedition was to follow, from C. Blanco eastward. The Uinta Mountains are the only mountain range in North America that lays West to East from the Sierra Nevada Mountains to the Rocky Mountains. The Spanish ruled over Mexico, New Spain, and Central America from 1542-1821, during this time of exploring and harvesting of precious metals there were a large population of Spaniards from the Uinta Basin south to Mexico. By unofficial accounts there were as many as 2000 conquistadors, protecting Spain's interests, i.e., the ancient mines found by the early Spanish expeditions, they also brought thousands of native slaves to mine the gold from the Uinta Mountains. Even today there are still signs of Spanish activity i.e., gold and copper smelters with cannon mounts, ruins of Spanish Missions in and around the Uinta Mountains.

During the 1760s, the Spaniards developed a fervent interest to explore the lands north of New Mexico and Arizona. The previously documented accounts from two centuries prior, in addition to the aspiration of expanding the Spanish Empire, prompted New Mexican authorities to send expeditions northward. Explorer Juan María Antonio Rivera was instructed by the government to explore the Río del Tizon, the Colorado River, and to learn the extent of Indian settlements in the north. Rivera and his party traveled along well-worn Spanish and Utah Indian-trader trails, moving northward into the Dolores River drainage in Colorado. In October of 1765, Rivera ventured into unfamiliar territory, crossing into Utah northeast of Monticello, and travelling into the Lisbon Valley and Spanish Valley.

In 1776, the year of the nation's declaration of independence. Catholic Fathers Francisco Atanasio Dominguez and Silvestre Velez de Escalante's Expedition came up from New Mexico in the south looking for a passage to the coast of California in 1776, they came north through country inhabited by Shoshone Indians they called 'Yutas' (a Spanish word for mountain dwellers) in Western Colorado. They crossed the Green River into the Uinta River Valley Basin in what is now the Uinta Valley Indian Reservation in Northeastern Utah where they stayed for several weeks to rest and graze their horses. There they met the Uinta-At Bands of Shoshone 'Yuta' who lived in the Uinta River Valley Basin at the foot of the Uinta Mountains and had Spanish horses since 1600. From there, they traveled west across the Uinta Basin to Heber City, west to the Timpanogos Mountains, down Provo Canyon, and into the Utah Lake area where they encountered the Timpanogos Bands of Yuta-Shoshone Indians who lived at the mouth of the canyon entering the Salt Lake Valley and what is now commonly called the Wasatch Front. They also met up with many other bands and family clans of Yuta and Shoshone Indians led by a headman or chief who were scattered throughout the West's Great Basin. The journal kept by the Fathers was the first written description of the Yuta-Shoshone lands and people residing throughout the West and in the Great Basin. Domínguez and Escalante gave Utah Valley the name of La Valle de Nuestra Señora de la Merced de los Timpanogos, describing the great valley and the lake of the Timpanogos as an inviting Spanish settlement with abundant resources and a docile and affable nation of Indians.

The Timpanogos had long established trade relations with the Mexicans. Utah's Antonga was the son of Chief Sanpitch. Escalante describes having, come in contact, with aboriginal peoples who were Snake-Shoshoni who called themselves "Timpanogostzis", an Aztecan-Shoshonian word meaning "People of the Rock water carriers" (referring to rock salt), whose leader was Turunianchi. Turunianchi had a son named Munch. Munch was the father of Sanpitch, Wakara, Arropeen, Tabby, Ammon, Sowiette, and Grospeen, who occupied a land that is now known as Utah. Dominguez named Mount Timpanogos, Timpanogos River (Provo River), Timpanogos Lake (Utah Lake) and Timpanogos Valley (Utah Valley) in honor of these people, an honor that remains to this day. who shared their knowledge of the area with the Domínguez–Escalante expedition in 1776. The expedition noted this topographical information and left without investigating further, as they were anxious to get home.[11]

Louis and Clark

The next notable expedition was the Lewis and Clark Expedition in 1805-1806. Sacajawea, a Shoshoni Indian woman and her French fur trader husband, Toussaint Charbonneau was hired in North Dakota to guide the Lewis and Clark expedition, she was pregnant at the time but her presence and that of her baby assured other Indians that this expedition was a peace mission and not a war party. Sacajawea spoke Shoshone, Siouan, and several dialects, she acted as a guide, translator, interpreter, and diplomat. The Lewis and Clark mission was to preempt the British claim to the Oregon Territory and to map and explore the lands between St. Lewis, Missouri, and the Pacific Ocean. The map they used had been drawn by a Siksika Indian for

---

11 Exploration of America, https://www.legendsofamerica.com

an employee of the Hudson Bay Fur Company and showed the entire Missouri River drainage system. Following the expedition, trappers began to move into the upper Missouri regions.

Etienne Provost

Then in 1824, explorer Etienne Provost entered what is now Utah and reported having, come in contact, with a Snake-Shoshone tribe (Timpanogos) living along the Timpanogos River (Provo River) and Timpanogos Lake. His party was attacked by Snake Indians on October 1824 at the Jordan River near its mouth at the Great Salt Lake. Eight men were lost, but Provost survived and established trading posts on the banks of both Utah Lake and the Great Salt Lake. From 1839 until his death in 1850, he continued to recruit and escort the employees of the fur company and various private expeditions, including John Audubon's natural history expedition of 1843.

John C. Fremont

John C. Fremont, an officer in the Topographical Corps of the United States, led five expeditions into the West. There is not a more recognizable name in early government explorations than John Charles Fremont. Although he traversed very little new ground in the west and used former mountain men as guides, his reports and maps provided much valuable information which stimulated westward migration. The 1843-44 expedition undoubtedly had the greatest impact. He surveyed the vast region he appropriately named the Great Basin and he traversed across the Salt Lake Desert. He recorded detailed descriptions of the soil, vegetation, wildlife, and the valleys as locations for future settlement. Fremont's enthusiastic description of the valley of the Great Salt Lake did much to encourage Brigham Young to bring the Mormons to the Great Basin to settle. Among the few government explorers not educated at West Point, Fremont came west for the first time in 1842, as far as the Wind River Mountains. In May 1843 he mounted a more ambitious, well-equipped exploration that would take him as far as Fort Vancouver in the Oregon country. While enroute to the northwest, he detoured south when he reached present-day Soda Springs and went through Cache Valley toward the Great Salt Lake. Following the Bear River to its mouth he was disappointed in not being able to get a good view of the lake. Fremont therefore went south to the Weber River to a point about six miles west of present-day Ogden, proceeded to Little Mountain, and climbed to its summit where he and his men could view the whole expanse of the lake. A few days later, Fremont's party, which included Kit Carson, reached an island (later designated "Fremont Island") from which they made a telescopic survey. They drew a map of the lake from a position on its rocky summit. Just below this point, the group carved what Carson called, "a large cross" on 9 September 1843. Though only seven inches long, it is visible on that rock formation to this day. Fremont also did a brief scientific analysis to determine the lake's salinity. After completing his trek to Fort Vancouver, Fremont journeyed south along the east slopes of the Sierra Nevada's searching for the mythical Buenaventura River. He confirmed the findings of the early mountain men that there was no channel that drained any of the Utah lakes into the Pacific Ocean. In 1844 Fremont left California and picked up the Old Spanish Trail, returning to the East via Utah Lake, Spanish Fork Canyon, and the Uinta Mountains. He was first to call the area that he had skirted during the years exploration; "The Great Basin."

In 1845 America's "Pathfinder" spent some more time in the Salt Lake Valley. On this trip, he discovered the relationship between the

Utah and Great Salt Lake with the connecting Jordan River. Again, with Kit Carson, he paid a visit to the large island which he named for its abundance of antelope. When he left the lake, he headed west across the Great Salt Lake Desert toward California, following a central route between those taken earlier by Jedediah Smith in 1827 and by Joseph Walker in 1833. Fremont's course would become a portion of the later Hastings Cut-off. He gave names to Pilot Peak and the Humboldt River in Nevada on this trip.

Fremont's final excursion through Utah was in 1853. It was a privately financed exploration to find a route for the proposed Pacific railroad. His course was, similar-to another undertaken earlier that year by Captain John W. Gunnison and was of little consequence to Utah's history compared to his earlier visits. However, it is interesting to note that he undertook this exploration, in an effort, to ascertain what the route would be like during the winter months. He entered present-day Utah by way of the Colorado River, and by the time he came through Fremont Pass and arrived in Parowan his entire party was suffering from hunger and exposure to the harsh winter conditions, having already lost one of their number in death. The residents took the survivors into their homes and nursed them back to health before they continued to California over the Old Spanish Trail.

Howard Stansbury

Howard Stansbury was accompanied by his second in command, Lieutenant J.W. Gunnison, and John Bridger as guide to lead an expedition in 1849 to the valley of the Great Salt Lake, this was the first federally funded government exploration guided by Bridger. His orders directed him to survey and map the Great Salt Lake Valley as well as; Utah Valley to evaluate the various emigrant roads in the area, including the Oregon Trail; It was designed to acquire geographical and geological data about the West that would facilitate a future route for a trans-continental railroad, the telegraph and to locate coal deposits. Bridger guided Stansbury's party east along trails that later became familiar as the Overland Trail and Union Pacific Railroad routes.

John Wesley Powell

John Wesley Powell developed an interest in the natural sciences as a young boy. After a continuing but intermittent education, losing an arm as he served with distinction in the Union Army during the Civil War, and becoming a professor of natural history, Powell turned his scientific attention to the American West. Although a former military man, he was one of the few government explorers not affiliated with the Corps of Engineers. He made preliminary visits to the Rockies and did land studies of the Colorado River before he began the exploration that would assure his place in history. He launched his famous voyage at Green River, Wyoming in 1869. Before his party of ten men and four boats floated as far as Uinta Valley to restock at the White Rocks Indian Agency on 6 July, they had already lost one boat in the treacherous canyon rapids. When Powell finished his trip down the Green and Colorado Rivers to the mouth of the Virgin River, he would lose another vessel and three of his men – killed by some Shivwits Indians who mistook them for troublesome prospectors. Many feared that the whole party had perished because for almost two months they were not seen by white men on their perilous journey through Desolation, Cataract, Glen, Marble, and Grand Canyons. Powell's party became the first to accomplish this journey. Two years later, this time with a sizable appropriation from Congress to map and explore the Colorado Plateau region, Powell repeated his river voyage as far as Lee's Ferry. This time he left the river to set up headquarters in Kanab, Utah. A year later, in August 1872, Powell's party again embarked (this time on a much higher Colorado River) but officially ended the second river expedition after passing through the dangerous Marble Canyon in Northern Arizona. While he continued his study of the plateau, Powell gave more place names to this region than anyone else except the Mormons.

His publications, *Exploration of the Colorado River* (1875), *Geology of the Uinta Mountains* (1876), and *Report on the Lands of the Arid Regions of the United States with a More Detailed Account of the Land of Utah* (1878), provided the necessary scientific information about the Colorado Plateau, particularly its geology and physical boundaries.

While Mormons began to settle the Utah region in 1847, scientific explorations continued. Of momentous importance were the expeditions conducted by John Wesley Powell. In 1867, John Wesley Powell, an appointed professor of geology, commenced a series of expeditions to the Rocky Mountains and the canyons of the Green and Colorado rivers. Powell and his party journeyed 900 miles with four boats, traveling from the Union Pacific Railroad crossing of the Green River in Wyoming down through the Grand Canyon.

CHAPTER 4:

Early Fur Trappers

Beginning in 1821, many fur-trading companies and individual trappers began to occupy the Rocky Mountains and Intermountain West, as insatiable American and European markets for fur and pelts flourished. In 1824, fur trappers, later referred to as mountain men, entered Utah from three directions. Americans enlisted with the William Ashley-Andrew Henry Fur Company came from St. Louis; the Hudson's Bay Company traveled from the north and northwest; and independent French-Canadian- American trappers journeyed from New Mexico, primarily Taos and Santa Fe. A group of Ashley-Henry trappers, under the lead of Jedediah Smith and Thomas Fitzpatrick, reached the upper Sweetwater River early in 1824 and turned westward to cross the Continental Divide by way of South Pass. Although South Pass had been traversed in 1812, the rediscovery of the pass represented a landmark for fur trappers, missionaries, gold rushers, and Mormons, as it became the major thoroughfare to the Great Basin. During the summer of 1824, John Weber, one of the most prominent members of the Ashley-Henry Fur Company, and his brigade crossed South Pass and Green River Valley and descended into the Bear River region and Cache Valley for the fall hunt. James Bridger, a member of John Weber's brigade, became a distinguished trapper, hunter, trader, and frontiersman.

The British Hudson's Bay Company, led by Peter Skene Ogden, set out from the company's Flathead Post in Montana on December 20, 1824. The brigade worked their way to the Bear River near the present site of Alexander, Idaho, and followed the river southward into Cache Valley. From the south end of Cache Valley, the brigade traversed into Ogden Valley. While Peter Skene Ogden and his brigade were traveling through Cache Valley, American trappers followed the Bear River to its mouth and explored southward along the front of the Wasatch Range.

As American and British fur companies were exploring the regions in northern Utah, Taos Trappers, including Etienne Provost and Antoine Robidoux, ranged into the San Juan, Colorado, Green, and Duchesne River drainages, and eventually voyaged into the Great Basin and Wasatch Mountains. In 1824, Etienne Provost, the most notable trapper operating from the Taos base in New Mexico, entered Utah by the same general route as Catholic missionary-explorers had in 1776. Provost followed the Duchesne River to the river that bears his name, the Provo River, and followed it to Utah Lake. Some historians affirm that Provost may have been the first Euro-American to see the Great Salt Lake.[12]

In May of 1825, a conflict and conspiracy between American and British trappers at Deserter Point on the Weber River forced Peter Skene Ogden to retreat to the Snake River. American trappers

---

12 Utah Historical Quarterly, Vol. 26, 1958, No. 4, MOUNTAIN MEN BEFORE THE MORMONS, By LeRoy R. Hafen.

continued to trap and trade in Utah even though the area legally belonged to Mexico. For over a decade, the Ashley-Henry Fur Company had tapped the richest fur areas in the West, and in turn, William Ashley developed a new system whereby fur supplies were brought to designated locations in the West. This social business activity became known as the annual rendezvous. The first rendezvous was held at Henry's Fork on the Green River; the next one in Cache Valley; the next two on the south end of Bear Lake; and the remainder were held in southwestern Wyoming and eastern Idaho until their discontinuance in 1840.

Through this wide-ranging activity, much of modern Utah was documented, described, and named. Renowned mountain men, including William Ashley, Jedediah Smith, John Weber, James Bridger, Peter Skene Ogden, and Etienne Provost, made significant contributions to the knowledge of the West by providing the foundation for later detailed exploration and mapping. Scientific and military expeditions conducted by John C. Fremont, John W. Gunnison, Howard W. Stansbury, and John Wesley Powell yielded detailed documentation of the Utah landscape.

In the Summer of 1828, Kentuckian William Reed teamed up with veteran fur trader Denis Julien to travel north from Taos into the Uinta Basin and establish the Reed Trading Post, a single cabin, at the confluence of the Whiterocks and Uinta Rivers. Reed and Julien were accompanied by William's twelve-year-old nephew, James Scott Reed. It is unknown whether they planned to trap, trade for the season, or set up permanent headquarters, but upon their entry into the area, they found enough success to warrant staying and building a trading post. The post remained in operation until 1832 when Antoine Robidoux bought the location and business from

Reed. After Robidoux purchased Reed's post, he built his fort about one-hundred yards to the north and west, to avoid the spring floods which had threatened the old location of the post every year. Fort Robidoux, also called Fort Uinta, Fort Winty, or Twinty, was located about 12 miles north-east of the present-day town of Roosevelt. The fort consisted of a small group of log cabins with dirt roofs and floors, surrounded by a log palisade. The enclosed area of the fort was about sixty by sixty feet, with gate openings at both the north and south ends. Robidoux's often ruthless business practices eventually aroused the wrath of the Yutas or Utahs and led to the destruction of Fort Uinta. As the beaver trade declined in the late 1830's and early 1840's, so too did Robidoux's business. In August 1844 Utah Shoshone Indians attacked and burned Fort Uinta. Causes for the attack could have included Robidoux's cheating of the Indians, involvement with the capture of Indian Women and Children for prostitution and slavery, and sales of guns and alcohol to the Utahs.

On June 30, 1834, Congress passed the Intercourse Act setting regulations and policy when dealing with Native Americans. Some of the features included that all people who traded with Indians had to be licensed, cattle could not be driven on Indian lands, no purchase or grants could be made with the Indians directly, any letters or messages sent to the Indians which caused trouble would be traced and the sender would be fined, any property of friendly Indians destroyed or damaged would be replaced or paid for by the one responsible, selling liquors to Indians was prohibited, Agents from the Government were in charge of executing these provisions. This act was later put into use in the Territory of Utah. In 1843 Jim Bridger, American fur trader, frontiersman, and scout, established Fort Bridger, in southwestern Wyoming, as a way station for emigrants traveling westward on the Oregon Trail and as a fur-trading post. Bridger was well known among the American Indian tribes of the Rockies, especially the Shoshone. Bridger's experience had few limits. He quit the dying fur trade in 1842 and in 1843, with his partner Louis Vasquez, established a trading post along the Blacks Fork of the Green River in what is now Wyoming and in what then was still a corner of Mexico. Bridger recognized that the overland migration to Oregon was a sign of changing settlement patterns, and that Fort Bridger could not help but become a profitable economic concern. For the next fifteen years, the post was a key supply point for Oregon, Mormon and California Trail emigrants needing provisions, livestock, and wagon repairs.[13]

---

13 The fort later served the U.S. Army, and it was not abandoned until 1890.) "Jim Bridger". Encyclopedia Britannica, 13 Mar. 2022, https://www.britannica.com/Jim-Bridger.

CHAPTER 5:

Military Campaigns

At the end of the Revolutionary War, 1775-1783, the Spanish began paying attention to the east and the new United States of America. The end of the Revolutionary War that saw the British being defeated and pushed off the continent. The Thirteen Colonies became the United States of America; and they were expanding west towards New Spain and the Pacific Ocean beyond.

In 1801, the Spanish realizing that times were changing, and the new United States of America would be wanting to expand, and they were in their way. Mexico rebelled against Spanish Rule and wanted to be free of Spain. Through rebellion and a change in Spanish royal leadership, Mexico was given more autonomy and was allowed to draft a constitution, the border was established between Mexico and New Spain, in about the area where the current day U.S. – Mexico border lies.

By 1803 the French no longer envisioned a sustained occupation off French soil. The French realized that the expense of such a Colony so far from home was more than they could afford, with political problems between France and Spain; the new United States of America was eager to expand its territory to the west and the French saw this as an opportunity to further assist the new government and entered the Louisiana Purchase for $15 million dollars. This purchase and transfer of lands doubled the size of the United States overnight, greatly strengthened the country materially and strategically and made it a gateway to the west. France made this deal without consulting Spain because Spain also claimed the westward portion of the Louisiana Territory as its sovereign lands, this didn't go well with Spain.

After the purchase of the Louisiana territory, Spain was making plans to return the New Spain territory to Mexico and withdraw from North and Central America. In 1821, Spain withdrew from all occupied lands and Mexico declared its independence from Spain. The former territory of New Spain now became New Mexico and Upper New California. During this time many Spanish citizens remained on lands granted to them by the King of Spain, their claims to those lands were recognized by the new Mexican Government and encouraged the Mexican people to move onto the newly acquired lands on newly issued government land grants.

By 1836, the Mexican government was losing their grip on New Mexico territory to the United States. Mexico was faltering after the capture of Mexican General Antonio Lopez De Santa Anna; he was taken prisoner by the Texas Army during the Texas Revolution. While being held prisoner Santa Anna was forced to sign the Velasco Treaty ceding Texas to the United States, a treaty which Mexico refused to acknowledge or honor.

In 1844, James K. Polk won the U.S. Presidential election on a platform to continue westward expansion to Oregon, Idaho, and Texas, although Utah was available for expansion it was not included in his promise to be opened for settlement. President Polk's policy was to advocate westward expansion by peaceful means or by armed force if necessary.

1845 Texas was officially declared annexed by the United States. By this time tensions were high between Mexico and the United States; war was on the horizon. Texas Territory was vast, the northern boundary followed the western side of the Rocky Mountains to the eastern end of the Uinta Mountains then south following what is current day Colorado-Utah state boundaries.

The Mexican American War lasted from 1846-1848 and was started because Mexico claimed Texas' border ended at Nueces River and the United States claimed Texas' ended at the Rio Grande Del Norte.

In 1846, President Polk met with eastern Mormon Church leaders. These church leaders met with the President at the request of Brigham Young to ask for government assistance to fund their continued westward migration, in an attempt, to escape persecution. It was at this meeting President Polk worked a deal for Brigham Young to get aid if he provided 500 Mormon volunteers to fight in the Mexican War.

President Polk established a U.S. Army "Mormon" Battalion consisting of 543 men, of which its members were of the same religious denomination, Mormon. This was unprecedented then and has never been repeated in the history of the United States Armed Forces. Officially the Mormon Battalion was designated the 1st Iowa Volunteers because the Mormons were in Iowa at the time President

Polk and Brigham Young came to their agreement for Mormons to fight in the war.

In early 1846 the battalion started its march from Council Bluff, Iowa to Santa Fe, New Mexico, the battalion was then to march to San Diego, California. While moving up the San Pedro River in Arizona the battalion was attacked, this battle was known as the "Battle of the Bulls" because it was a herd of wild cattle that attacked the battalion, many bulls were killed, and two soldiers were wounded. During their march to San Diego, they encountered "NO" Mexican forces nor did they engage in any battles of the war. On the activation of the Mormon Battalion, Brigham Young had prophesied that not a single Mormon soldier would be lost to hostile action, he knew ahead of time that they would not be engaging in any hostile forces, their mission was to lead a trail to California.

By January 1848 Mexico had requested its people living in New Mexico return to Mexico because they were getting ready to surrender all interest and or claim to the lands of New Mexico and Upper California. At this request, a large number, of people abandoned their lands and returned to Mexico, but many stayed behind on their land grants. In February 1848, Treaty of Guadalupe Hidalgo was signed by representatives of the United States and Mexico ending the two-year war. The treaty contains 23 Articles, Article 10 was stricken leaving 22 Articles agreed upon by both countries. In the agreement the United States paid Mexico $15 million dollars for 525,000 square miles of land. These lands became California, Nevada, Arizona, New Mexico, Texas, Colorado, and Utah. At the end, of the Mexican American War in 1848 the majority of the U.S. Army Mormon Battalion were discharged, and the Battalion disbanded.[14]

---

14 Commissioner of Indian Affairs Report, October 1, 1861, Dyman S. Wood, Superintendent to Major H. Martin, "Utah Superintendency".

Articles IX and XI of the Treat of Guadalupe Hidalgos were specifically regarded by Mexico as not negotiable and mandatory to make the treaty acceptable.

Article IX: This article pertains to former Mexican citizens and the land grants by the Mexican Government and the previous Spanish Government that were recognized by Mexico.

Article IX: The Mexicans who, in the territories aforesaid, shall not preserve the character of citizens of the Mexican Republic, conformably with what is stipulated in the preceding article, shall be incorporated into the Union of the United States. and be admitted at the proper time (to be judged of by the Congress of the United States) to the enjoyment of all the rights of citizens of the United States, according to the principles of the Constitution and in the meantime shall be maintained and protected in the free enjoyment of their liberty and property and secured in the free exercise of their religion without restriction.

Special Note: The United States Government did not honor this article and the land grants were dissolved and the lands were opened for homesteading during the U.S. Westward Expansion.

Article XI: These articles pertain to the "savage tribes" that inhabit the ceded lands. The Arapaho, Apache, Comanche, Utahs and Shoshone in particular, were to become the responsibility of the United States Government to keep these tribes from conducting raids against Mexico, Mexican citizens, and their property. To restrain and prosecute Indians and non-Indians from the bartering of slaves between the United States and Mexico.

The reason this Article was so important to the Mexican Government is because for years the "savage tribes" burned out settlers, stole cattle, murdered, and kidnapped Spanish and Mexican settlers, they were sold/traded or made slaves of the tribe(s). They also continuously harassed the Spanish/Mexican military forces in New Mexico and Upper California.

The "savage tribes" they referred to were the Arapaho, Apache, Comanche, Navajo, Utahs and Shoshone (the Utah and Shoshonean tribes claimed aboriginal lands from the Rocky Mountains west to the Pacific Ocean, north to Canada and south to Mexico); these tribes were defiant against both the Spanish and the Mexican occupation of their ancestorial lands and fought them at every turn. Both the Spanish and Mexicans feared these warrior tribes and could not control them, nor could they defeat them, they were likely very pleased to finally be rid of them.

The Civil War (April 12, 1861, to April 9, 1865): Influenced Utah Territory's Indian policy in ways that could not have been envisioned at the beginning of the war. Utah's geographic isolation diminished in October 1861 when the telegraph reached Salt Lake City and linked the nation together. When the soldiers stationed in Utah were withdrawn in 1861 to fight the war in the East, the telegraph lines, mail lines, and emigrant trails, as well as the citizens who lived within the territory were left with little protection. With the telegraph's arrival, Utah's new superintendent for Indian Affairs, Dyman S. Wood, warned Washington officials that the "establishment of the overland daily mail and telegraph lines, and their recent completion through this Territory – consummations of such vital importance to the people throughout the Union – render it necessary that steps should be immediately taken by the government to prevent the possibility of their being interrupted by the Indians."[15]

---

15 U.S. Military History, https://www.military.com

New York Times (New York)
7 SEPTEMBER 1862

"Affairs in Utah," – It was into that tense environment that U.S. Army California Volunteers under the command of Colonel Connor entered Utah in late fall 1862 and established Camp Douglas on the foothills overlooking Salt Lake City. An eastern newspaper reported that Colonel Connor's "particular business is generally understood to be to keep the Western mail and emigrant route clear of Indians." One contributing factor to Connor's dislike of the Mormon is that he believed Latter-day Saints encouraged and instigated Indian raids throughout his area of responsibility. "Mormons," Connor complained to his superiors, "instead of assisting to punish Indians for bad conduct it actually encouraged them." From the evidence before me I am well satisfied that the Mormons are the real instigators."[16]

New York Times (New York)
30 JUNE 1865

"From Utah" – "What to do with the red men is still a problem which, it appears, cannot be satisfactorily solved. For this Spring there seems to be as much chance of difficulties with them, all around, as ever. We hear of Indian troubles from every quarter nearly." "Indians here, as elsewhere, dwindle away before the onward march of the white man. Chief after chief is passing away from the small Utah bands, until it is said to be difficult to find eligible and aspiring braves to fill the vacancies." What happened in Utah when settlers and Indians came into contact is the same story that occurred throughout the early history of the United States. Settlers arrived, they took lands, murdered &

---

16 *Report of Brig. Gen. P. Edward Connor, April 9, 1863. While the Civil War ended in 1865, Utah's Indian problems did not. Toward the conclusion of the Civil War, a Utah-based New York Times reporter complained.*

starved the Indians, and then displaced those who survived. In Utah Territory it happened quickly. From the arrival of the first Mormon pioneers, it was just over thirty years until the last Indians were removed to government reservations.[17]

17 U.S. History Primary Source Timeline- Library of Congress, https://www.loc.gov

CHAPTER 6:

Utahs and Shoshone

The Yuta-Shoshone Nation and its many divisions still occupy a vast swath of the West. Today, the Northern Shoshone is concentrated in eastern Idaho, western Wyoming, and northeastern Utah; the Western Shoshone is in Nevada, western Idaho, southeast Oregon, northwestern Utah, and California; the Eastern Shoshone (the only group of the three to fully-adopt the Plains Indian lifestyle) is in Wyoming, Montana, the Uinta Basin in northeastern Utah and the landed area in Utah reaching to the crest of the Rocky Mountains in western Colorado.

Notable Leaders and Treaties

Chief Washakie (The Rattle 1798-1900). Chief of the Eastern Shoshone in Wyoming, Washakie was first mentioned in 1840 in the journal of American fur trapper Osborne Russell. Washakie led his band of Shoshone to the council meetings in Wyoming that resulted in the Treaty of Fort Laramie in 1851 and the Wind River Reservation.

They used the horse to hunt the buffalo/bison that grazed west of the Continental Divide, on the Great Plains. In 1897 Washakie was baptized an Episcopalian. He died three years later at Flathead Village in Montana's Bitterroot Valley and was buried with full military honors at Fort Washakie, Wyoming.

Chief Pocatello (Tondzaosha – Buffalo Robe 1815-1884). Shoshone leader led many attacks against early settlers during a time of friction between whites and Native Americans in the Great Basin. Pocatello led his people to their present reservation in southern Idaho, where they were relocated on land that was much more conducive to horse raising and subsequently abandoned much of their earlier traditions in favor of adopting Spanish "horse culture". Like the Shoshone in Wyoming, they used the horse to hunt the buffalo/bison that grazed west of the Continental Divide, on the Great Plains. After his death in 1884, Pocatello's body was interred in a deep spring in Idaho along with his clothing, guns, knives, and hunting equipment. Eighteen horses were also slaughtered and put into the spring on top of his body.

Chief Tabby-To-Qwana (1814-1902). Chief Tabby led his bands of Yuta-Shoshone from the Great Basin and the Mormons in 1861 to the Uinta River Valley Basin Reservation in northeastern Utah that was established by President Abraham Lincoln by Executive Order to keep the Mormons out of the Uinta Basin and to protect the Utahs from further decimation. Chief Anterro and his people, the Uinta-Ats had occupied the Uinta Basin since before the 1100's and had Spanish horses since 1600. Chief Tabby-To-Qwana died October 27, 1902 in his home north of the Whiterocks Indian Village on the Uinta Valley Reservation in Utah. The Yuta-Shoshone is the leading Nation of native people who are inter-related, with slightly different Shoshonean linguistic dialects and traditions, that occupied a vast area of land in the high desert regions between the Sierra Nevada Mountains in the west and the Rocky Mountains in the east that stretched out to the Great Plains. Covering a landed area that is now the States of Nevada, Utah, Oregon, Idaho, Montana, Wyoming, California, Arizona, and Colorado; territory that was at that time, (1800) claimed by the Republic of Mexico. The territory described had been home to these indigenous natives of the Great Basin for thousands of years; (as far back as the Ancient Freemont Culture where early residents lived in caves or rock shelters in 6000 B.C. and whose petroglyphs and arti-facts are found all over in the Great Basin States and the Uinta Valley Basin in northeastern Utah and western Colorado).

The Shoshone Nation occupied Utah Territory long before it was invaded by the Mormon settlers in 1847 and long before it was ceded by the Republic of Mexico to the United States in 1848 under the Treaty of Guadalupe Hidalgo. Although the Indian bands and tribes of Shoshone people were, at this time, very numerous, the word "Yutas" was regularly applied by European migrants, trappers, settlers, and Mormons, to those located south of the Great Salt Lake, and 'Shoshone or Snakes' to those located north and west of the Lake, especially in the Valley of the Humboldt River. The 'Snakes' and 'Yutas', however, were all Shoshone bands with slightly different linguistic dialects, lifestyles, traditions, and one ancient Mesoamerica origin.

Background

Brigham Young and his followers entered the Salt Lake Valley of the Great Basin in 1847 looking for a place to settle outside the United States where they could practice their form of religion undisturbed. The Republic of Mexico held ceded territorial rights to the entire region as far northward as the Great Salt Lake, westward to the Coast of California and eastward to the summit of the Rocky Mountains. The year after the Mormons arrived in the Salt Lake Valley of the Great Basin, the United States and the Republic of Mexico settled their war over the territorial rights to the Western Empire claimed by the Republic of Mexico. The dispute had resulted in the Mexican American War of 1848. Mexico was defeated and the United States took possession of the empire pursuant to the Treaty of Guadalupe Hidalgo whereby the Yuta-Shoshone Nation and the Mormon settlers came under the jurisdiction of the United States. The United States began creating territories out of the newly acquired lands. Utah Territory was established in 1850 to include all the area west of the Rocky Mountains stretching into Shoshone Territory west across the Great Basin area to the State of Nevada and California. The Uinta Band of Yuta-Shoshone Indians hold aboriginal ("Indian Title") title to over fifty-five million acres of land crossing the Salt Lake Valley in Utah into the Nevada border and south into Arizona. With the westward expansion, there was considerable demand for the extinguishment of Indian Title in Utah. The Uinta River Valley Reservation was established in 1861 for the purpose of protecting the tribes of Utahs and to keep the Mormons out of the Uinta River Basin in northeastern Utah. The Yuta-Shoshone Indians were often mis-identified by the Mormons who called them "Utes" when they arrived in the Valley for the first time. In a short time, problems developed as Mormon occupation expanded south into Utah Valley and when Fort Utah was constructed on the central campground of the Tum-pan-u-wach Band of Shoshone Indians, resistance broke out followed by many deprivations committed by the Europeans to chase the Indians away.

By proclamation, in 1850, the first Governor of Utah Territory, Brigham Young, divided the territory into three agencies; the "Uinta

Agency" to include all Shoshone or Snake Bands of Pah-Vant, San-Pitch, Tim-pa-noys, Cummum-bah, Tumpanawach, Uinta-At 'Yuta', and the Uinta Yampa (not to be confused with the Colorado Uintah Yampah who are a mixture of Comanche and Arapaho) and other fragments of Yuta-Shoshone Indian bands and family clans of Utah Territory.

During 1853-54, there occurred what was known as the Walker War. Wakara was a favorite war chief of the 'Yuta' or Utah. He had three well-known brothers: Arapeen, San-Pitch, and Tabby-To-Qwanah and lessor known half-brothers Ammon, Grospine, Young Uinta, Battease, Tobiob (The Clouds), Penunktum Uinta and Namutum Uinta. Walkara also and two sisters Parumputs Jane Towats and Tahvap Dora Copperfield and a half-sister Viroque Uinta. Wakara was in the prime of his life. In addition to several of the Native dialects, he could converse fluently in Spanish and make himself understood in English. Before the coming of the Mormons, he made frequent raids into towns throughout Mexico, looting and taking captives for ransom, the slave trade, and stealing many horses. He was a wealthy man by Indian standards. At first Wakara received the exiled Mormon saints, with open arms, he gave them information as to the nature of the country, advised them where to establish settlements, and guarded them from depredation. But when he saw that they had occupied his choicest lands; when game disappeared from the canyons and mountain sides; and when his people were shot down without provocation, and their cattle stolen by bands of emigrants, his friendship turned to hostility and anger, and he longed to rid himself of the white man. The Walker War lasted approximately two years. The Native people were mercilessly pushed by the Mormons south within said Utah Territory and east of the eastern rim of the Great Basin into the desert area located in the east and northeastern half of the State of Utah - the Uinta Basin - that includes Ashley Valley were the Shoshone Uinta-ats have lived from time immemorial within the Uinta River Basin an area that joins the western border of the State of Colorado and runs 60 miles inward to the crest of the Rocky Mountains.

On October 3, 1861, President Abraham Lincoln created the Uinta Valley Reservation in the Uinta River Valley Basin. The area of the reservation recommended in the October 03, 1861, letter from Secretary of the Interior Smith approved by President Lincoln in creating the reserve "as of yet, unoccupied by settlement of our citizens." It included "the entire Valley of the Uinta River within Utah Territory, extending on both sides of said river to the crest of the first range of contiguous mountains on each side..." An area of approximately 5.5 million acres of mostly high desert land "for the permanent settlement and exclusive occupancy" of the tribes of Utah Territory, located in the northeastern corner of what is now the State of Utah. The Uinta Valley Basin Reservation was confirmed by Congress on May 5, 1864 (13 Stat. 63). The Yuta-Shoshone Indians who settled and stayed on the reservation after 1861 lost their previous 'band' identity as they were forced into the reservation and subsequently amalgamated as the "Uinta Band" (a.k.a., Uinta Valley Shoshone Tribe of 'Yuta' Indians). A geographic location name given to them by Indian agents of the time. The natives at the Uinta Agency are not ethnically identified as Shoshone Indians but just as the "Uinta Band" after 1861.

On the 7th day of August 1855, chief Wakara died, and the leading spirit of the Yuta-Shoshone left their midst. He was succeeded by his brother Arapeen; Arapeen was succeeded by San-Pitch, who was succeeded by Tabby-To-Qwanah who was afterward chief of the Yuta-Shoshone or Utahs. It was chief Tabby who led his people, headed by several sub-chiefs, to the Uinta River Valley Basin Reservation in northeastern Utah after it was set apart from the public domain in 1861. The spelling variation of the word 'Yuta' or 'Utah' depends on who is doing the spelling but in-any-case, it means Shoshone Indian.[18]

---

18 Commissioner of Indian Affairs Reports 1849 – 1878, The National Archives

CHAPTER 7:

There Are No Utes in Utah

The ancient Proto-Shoshonean language is not a Numic language branch of the so-called Uto-Aztecan language family that claims over 30 known languages found almost exclusively in Western United States and Mexico. The term "Uto-Aztecan" suggests the conjoining of the "Ute" language of Utah and the ancient Aztecan languages of Mexico, which is directly associated with the Aztec people of Mexico and South America. If the nuche, we know today as "Utes" have any kind of ancient archeological history it derives through the evolution of the Paleo-Indians who migrated from Alaska (825-1000 A.D.) south to California, Arizona, and New Mexico. Over time these Paleo-Indian groups divided into two linguistically distinct people, the Navajo, and Apache (Jicarilla, Mescalero, Chiricahua, Western Apache) with whom the "Utes" are closely aligned. Sometimes these cultures are referred to as the Southwestern Athabascan or Apachean people, they settled areas adjacent to the Anasazi Culture in New Mexico and Arizona around A.D. 400.[19]

---

19 Indians of North America: Selected Resources – Library of Congress, https://www.loc.gov

Much misinformation has been widely distributed about the location and origin of what is known today as the Ute People in Utah. There is no archeological evidence of any nature found that indicates the Mesoamerica cultures that inhabited the Great Basin during the period of the Fremont Culture and into the 19th century are from the same group origins as today's people called "Utes." A.D. 1600 is the first mention of "Utes" in general history of Arizona. The word "Ute" was first used by the early Spanish explorers, (Coronado - 1540) it is a Spanish word meaning 'unknown' or 'unknown Indian'; "Spanish kidnapped Apache, Navajos, and Utes (implies a mix) who lived near Spanish colonies in New Mexico to use as slave labor or household servants." In the 1850's the Mormon settlers in Utah Territory used the word as a derogatory slur for all Native Americans and the Indian Agents erroneously used the term, at times, in their reports to Commissioners on Indian Affairs particularly after 1880. The word "Ute" was never applied to any band, group, or tribe of Indians until the United States government coined the word "Ute" and applied it in a treaty creating the tribe of Confederated Bands of "Ute" Indians of Colorado in 1868. The seven bands involved consisted of three bands of Yamparika, Parianuche, and Uintah ("White Rivers") and four bands of mixed Mexican/Paiute/Apache natives identified by the United States Agents as: Southern[20] Ute (Moache); Ute Mountain Ute (Weeminuche), White Mesa Ute (Scheberetch), and Tabaquache Ute (Uncompahgre).

The people we know today as Uncompahgre, Southern Ute, White Mesa Ute, and Ute Mountain Ute are not a stand-alone band that can reasonably be labeled as "unknown." They consisted of small mixed families of Mexican/Apache/ Southern Paiute Natives. They largely inhabited lands in the Southern States we know today as the

---

20 Commissioner of Indian Affairs Reports 1849 – 1878, The National Archives

Southwest Region of the United States; they historically roamed from Southern California to Eastern New Mexico and Mexico. The Uncompahgre Ute were inter-married with the Jicarilla Apache in New Mexico where they were known as the Tabaquache Paiutes, also known as Mo-wa-to-ve-wach and Pobawotche (Southern Paiutes). They frequented the Great Plains, Texas, and areas of Mexico, but never ventured further north to hunting grounds than Southern Utah. "They are subdivided into several small bands under petty chiefs, who acknowledge no superior, and roam over a vast extent of country, having no permanent place of residence, and hence are often difficult to be found." [Commissioner of Indian Affairs Report No.84 (1854).]

These natives relocated to Colorado from New Mexico by Treaty agreement in 1863. The Treaty signed by seven chiefs of the Uncompahgre Utes on October 7, 1863, called for all New Mexico Ute bands to relinquish, among other things, all mountain areas settled by whites in Colorado. The Uncompahgre Ute were to be located near Conejos in southern Colorado in exchange for signing the treaty. The treaty included territory of the three bands of White Rivers who were not in attendance at the treaty counsel. This treaty and the treaty of 1864 was superseded by the treaty of March 2, 1868, with the "Confederated Bands of "Ute" Indians of Colorado". Whereby they agreed to share a 15-million-acre reservation located in 1/3rd of Western Colorado Territory; bordered on the west by the Rocky Mountains.

The White River Utes are a mixture of Comanche and Arapaho who were historically closely associated with the Southern Paiute Bands long before they shared a land base in Colorado. The connection between these bands was Chief Colorow (or Colorado). He was born a Comanche in 1813. When he was 5 years old his family was hunting, in the area, of New Mexico, when they were attacked by Southern Paiutes. He was captured and raised by the Southern Paiute (Moache) and eventually he married three sisters from the Yampah Comanche tribe. His affiliation with the Comanche brought the three White River bands and the four Southern Paiute bands into a closer relationship as the Confederated Bands of "Ute" Indians of Colorado in 1868. In summary, the United States government set apart a 15-million-acre reservation, by treaty, in 1868 for the Confederated Bands of 'Unknown' Indians of Colorado, whereby the Indians agreed to relinquish all claims to all other lands in the United States not included in the said reservation that was established in the Western 1/3rd of what is now the State of Colorado.

Eleven years (1879) after the Confederated Bands of Colorado Utes signed the 1868 Treaty, the White River Utes attacked the agency on the White River in Colorado and killed Indian Agent Nathan C. Meeker in Northwestern Colorado and his 10 male employees for plowing up a horse pasture used by the Indians. The Indians took the Agent's wife and child along with other women and children as hostages. As the White Rivers fled south an infantry of U. S. Army Soldiers went in pursuit, there was an attack at Mill Creek on the Soldiers led by Major Thomas T. Thornburgh, killing the Major and 13 troops before they could rescue the captives. This incident enraged the Colorado Senators, settlers, and prospectors who applied political pressure that caused the United States to withdraw the Tribe's claims to the 15-million-acre reservation and the subsequent expulsion of the White River and Uncompahgre Ute bands from Colorado Territory and relocated them 'temporarily' for their safety to Utah Territory until suitable land was found in Colorado for them to settle upon permanently as allottees. The Meeker Massacre, as well as other political factors prompted the 1880 action in Congress to force the break-up of the Confederated Ute Indian Bands as the cry "The

Utes must go" from the white settlers and miners was raised urging the removal of the Utes from Colorado.

In December of 1879, a Joint Resolution was introduced to Congress to authorize the Secretary of the Interior to declare the Ute Indian's rights to their reservation forfeited if the tribe did not deliver the Indians engaged in the White River and Mill Creek massacres. This was one of several bills and resolutions introduced to Congress calling for the expulsion of the Utes from Colorado; permanent forfeiture of reservation lands; and various other sanctions that included their consent to cede all lands to the United States that remained of the reservation established by the Treaty of March 2, 1868, in exchange for allotments located in designated areas in Colorado and consent to be subject to the civil and criminal laws of "the State in which they may reside" thereafter.

There were no "Utes" (by that name) historically indigenous to the Great Basin or the Salt Lake Valley in the Territory of Utah prior to 1880. The bands of Paiute Indians who are part of the Confederated Ute Bands of Colorado would not arrive in Colorado Territory until 1863 from New Mexico Territory. Subsequently these four bands of Southern Paiutes were joined with the three small bands of White Rivers that are mixed Comanche/Arapaho Plains Indians and the seven bands were combined by the United States to create a tribe of Confederated Bands of "Ute" Indians of Colorado. Two of these bands, (White River and Uncompahgre) did not arrive in Utah from Colorado Territory until 1881. This chronology of a culture and historic events indicates the people we know as "Ute" are not actually "Ute" and are not historically indigenous to Colorado, Utah, or the Great Basin.[21]

---

21 Handbook of American Indians North of Mexico. Hodge, Frederick Webb, Government Printing Office, Washington DC Publication Date: 1910.

CHAPTER 8:

The Mormons

The Mormon (Latter-day Saints) Pioneer Company arrived at Fort Bridger on July 7, 1847. They spent a day there; but found all the prices very inflated. When a small group of Mormons settled nearby, tensions began to mount between Bridger and the new settlers. The settlers reported to Brigham Young, that Bridger was selling liquor and ammunition to the Indians, in violation of federal law.

On July 24, 1847, Mormon (Latter-day Saints) pioneers entered the Great Salt Lake Valley from Emigration Canyon. The westward migration was prompted when the towns people of Nauvoo, Illinois stopped the Mormons attempt, to take over the town, to create a theocratic government under Mormon rule. In a theocratic system, God was to be the ultimate power and would give law to the people which they would be free to accept or reject, presumably based on republican principles. There was no democracy in Nauvoo, Joseph Smith was not only president of the Church; he was mayor, head of the municipal court, and general of the militia. He ran for President of the United States in 1844 advocating for a "theocracy". He wrote, "I go emphatically, virtuously, and humanely, for a Theocracy, where God and the people hold the power to conduct the affairs of men in righteousness." The townspeople also would not tolerate their young daughters being enticed from their homes to practice polygamy. The Mormons disregard culminated in the assassination of their prophet and leader, Joseph Smith. The new prophet of the Mormon Church (Church of Jesus Christ of Latter-day Saints), Brigham Young, made a definitive commitment to move west when it became apparent that the Mormons could not peacefully survive in Nauvoo, Illinois. The Great Salt Lake Valley was chosen as an isolated location in Mexico where they could practice their faith in comparative freedom. A new power was growing and resisting federal authority.

"In addition to this, and to co-operate with it, it has been made known by revelation, that it will be pleasing to the Lord, should they form a matrimonial alliance with the Natives; and by this means the Elders, who comply with the thing so pleasing to the Lord, and for which the Lord has promised to bless those who do it abundantly, gain a residence in the Indian territory, independent of the agent. It has been made known to one, who has left his wife in the state of N.Y. that he is entirely free from his wife, and he is at liberty to take him a wife among the Lamanites (Native Americans). It was easily perceived that his permission was perfectly suited to his desires. I have frequently heard him state, that the Lord had made it known to him, that he is as free from his wife as from any other woman; and the only crime that I have ever heard alleged against her is, she is violently opposed to Mormonism."[22]

---

22 Ezra Booth, Ohio Star, December 8, 1831)

"We are now going to the Lamanites (Native Americans), to whom we intend to be messengers of instruction. We will show them that in consequence of their transgressions a curse has been inflicted upon them, in the darkness of their skins. We will have intermarriages with them, they marry our young women, and we take their young squaws to wife. By these means it is the will of the Lord that the curse of their color shall be removed, and they restored to their pristine beauty."[23]

The following year, the United States acquired the entire region of the Great Basin from the Republic of Mexico by the Treaty of Guadalupe Hidalgo in 1848 and the Mormons were back under the laws of the United States.

The Mormon invasion of the Great Basin in 1847 was followed by two decades of anomalous Indian-white relations. Not-withstanding petitions to Congress from the Territorial Legislative Assembly, native title to the domain was not extinguished and the government delayed establishment of a land office in Utah until 1869. In the meantime, the Saints occupied every Indian homeland on the eastern border of the basin. In the absence of congressional action, Brigham Young, as Indian superintendent from 1850 to 1857, together with Garland Hurt, established several "Indian Farms," or little reservations, designed to introduce the natives to agriculture. The most important of these was located at Spanish Fork in Utah Valley.

Brigham Young and his followers entered the Salt Lake Valley of the Great Basin, claimed by the Republic of Mexico. In what is now Western Utah, they were looking for a place to settle outside the United States where they could practice their form of religion undisturbed. The Republic of Mexico held ceded territorial rights to

---

23 Prophet Brigham Young, quoted in The Abominations of Mormonism Exposed.

the entire region as far northward as the Great Salt Lake, westward to the Coast of California and eastward to the summit of the Rocky Mountains. The Shoshone Indians living in the area were mis-identified by the Mormons who called them "Utes" when they arrived in the Valley for the first time. The Castilian Spanish word "Ute" was commonly used by the Mexicans at that time to identify unknown individual Indians as evidenced by some of their writings. It was not used to identify a Shoshone Tribe or band of Indians they collectively called "Yuta's." Problems developed as the Mormon occupation expanded.

As Great Basin bands encountered the Spanish and other Europeans, they adjusted their mode of gathering necessary resources based on new technologies, such as horses and guns, as well as their myths to cope with change. This process entailed some adjustment in their perceptions of the world around them and in their own perception of their identities. Some Indigenes, such as the Utes and Comanches, raided other Native bands throughout the Southwest enslaving women and children who they traded to the Spanish in exchange for additional horses and guns. Native American children, acquired through this difficult and wrenching raid-and-trade process, experienced a major cultural shift that imposed upon them an external identity. They reacted to that shift in varied ways that expressed individual constructed identity.

The Utahs and others who sold, traded, or gave them away, and the Mormons who purchased, accepted, or received them in trade, struggled to define rules governing the practice and their obligations concerning the children caught up by that practice individual personality characteristics, preconceived notions about the opposing culture, and the external actions of the United States federal government, complicated rules definition and the subsequent behavior of those involved. Over four-hundred children lived in Mormon homes in North America's Great Basin between 1847 and the early 1900s. The children came to Mormon households as captives, or as a traded commodity, the result of intricate, wrenching, sometimes deadly cultural conflicts and negotiations between their own people and the Mormons. Mormons purchased children as slaves for a variety of reasons: because they wanted children, because they felt they needed to be civilized, because they wanted to convert them. Child slaves soon became a vital source of labor for the settlers, some of whom traded them to other Mormons or even gave them as gifts. Utah Indians, many of whom were starving, sold their children to Mormon people in order too, ensure their survival.

The Mormons attempted to Anglicize the children, and "imposed a new order and identity" on them. There were also three black slaves that came along with the original Mormon settlers, and with an 1852 law legalizing slavery in Utah, other Mormons followed suit. By 1850, two-thirds of the around 100 black people in Utah were slaves. The same paternalistic attitudes that drove indigenous slavery among the Mormons were applied to black slaves, and once Utah determined it would be a slaveholding territory in 1852, even more slave owners entered the state.

As an official slave territory, Utah regulated both the African and Native slave trades. Native American slaves were "indentured" for 20 years; black slaves until they could "satisfy the debt" their master had incurred to purchase them. Slave owners were also required to educate and punish their slaves. The laws held a double standard; black slaves were handled more harshly than Native American ones. In 1862 Congress outlawed slavery in all United States territories, including Utah. Most black slaves, now free, moved out of the state. Meanwhile, many Native people stayed with the families they had lived with during slavery. Some assimilated, though few married Mormons due to taboos against mixed-race marriages; others went back to what remained of their families of origins and tried to reintegrate into Native society. (Mixed-race marriage was illegal.)

Historians still argue about whether the church is culpable for engaging in a slave trade that most Mormons recognized as evil and tried to curb. But intentions are not outcomes, and the consequences of Mormons' willingness to tolerate slavery in Utah can still be felt today. Though slavery technically ended in Utah in 1862, the church's attempt to convert Native Americans did not.[24]

Although the Indian bands and tribes of Shoshone people were, at this period, very numerous, the word "Yutas" was regularly applied to those located south of the Great Salt Lake, and 'Shoshone or Snakes' to those located north and west of the Lake, especially in the Valley of the Humboldt River. The 'Snakes' and 'Yutas', however, were both Shoshone Tribes.

The Uinta Valley Shoshone bands of 'Yutas' are erroneously referred to by Utah settlers and Mormon attorneys throughout many 1900 judicial proceeding as "Ute" regardless that all the surrounding history is clear that the original "Uinta Band of Yuta Indians" to settle on the Uinta River Valley Basin Reservation in northeastern Utah are Yuta and Shoshone Indians who were pushed out of the Salt Lake Valley by Brigham Young and his Mormon settlers after 1847. This error in identification is partly responsible for the bootstrapping scheme carried out by the State of Utah and the Confederated Bands

---

24 Cannon, Brian Q. "Adopted or Indentured, 1850-1870: Native Children in Mormon Households", in Nearly Everything Imaginable: The Everyday Life of Utah's Mormon Pioneers, ed. Ronald W. Walker et al. (Provo, Utah: Brigham Young University Press, 1999), 341-357.)

of Ute Indians of Colorado et al., in 1954. The false implication is that the Uinta Valley Shoshone Indians of the Uinta River Valley Basin Reservation are somehow, "Ute" Indians and they are a part of the Confederated Bands of Ute Indians of Colorado. The United States Claims Court in 1957, however, found this not to be the case.

The Uinta River Valley Reservation was established in 1861 for the purpose of keeping the Mormons out of the Uinta River Valley. With the westward expansion, there was considerable demand for the extinguishment of Indian Title in Utah. The Uinta Band of 'Yuta' Shoshone Indians sufficiently proved to the Court, it holds "Indian Title" to over 55-million acres of land crossing the Salt Lake Valley in Utah into the Nevada border and south into Arizona. The demand for extinguishment of Indian title culminated in an Act of Congress authorizing the negotiation of the "Spanish Fork Treaty" in June 1865. Under the terms of that treaty the Indians who were parties thereto, agreed to give up a defined area which included the land presently claimed and much more; Utah Territory then being considerably larger than the present State of Utah. By this unratified treaty, the Uinta Valley Reservation previously established in 1861 was again confirmed in 1957 as reserved to the Uinta Valley Shoshone Indians. The Court also issued two Interlocutory Decrees that were never followed by the United States Government; to submit to the Court documents of proof that the United States had purchased the lands, identified to the Court, by treaty from the Uinta Band. Until this verification was submitted to the Court, the Uinta Band of Yuta Indians hold the 'aboriginal title' to said federal lands crossing the Salt Lake Valley identified in the 1865 Unratified Spanish Fork Treaty.

Peace Treaty at Albuquerque, NM – The natives inhabiting the area within the territory ceded by Mexico were included in this peace treaty. It did not apparently deal specifically with the Uinta Valley Shoshone Indians. No reservation or land ownership was created, but the treaty recognized the Indians' right to occupy certain lands within the area that later became the territories of Colorado, New Mexico, and Utah. Specific boundaries are not described and were to be determined in the future. This treaty was ratified by Congress on September 9, 1850. By this treaty the natives in Utah Territory acknowledged themselves under jurisdiction of the United States of America. The treaty was signed at Albuquerque, NM. The signing did not include the Shoshone bands of 'Yuta' Indians from the Salt Lake Valley or the Uinta River Valley Basin east thereof.

Letter, John Wilson – Fort Bridger, Black's Fork on Green River or Colorado River

22 AUGUST 1849

Sir: We have arrived here yesterday. Messrs. Vasquez and Bridger are the proprietors and have resided here and in these mountains for more than twenty-five years. They are engaged as traders, belonging to the American Fur Company. They are gentlemen of integrity and intelligence and can be fully relied on in relation to any statement they make in regard, to the different tribes, claims, boundaries, and other information in relation to the Utah (Yuta) and Sho-sho-nie tribes, and a small band of Bannocks, as they have during all their residence, been engaged in trade with them. Among the Sho-sho-nies there are two bands, properly speaking. The principal or better portion are called Sho-sho-nies, or Snakes, who are rich enough to own horses; the others, the Sho-sho-ko, or Walkers, or those who cannot or do not own horses. The principal Chiefs of the Sho-sho-nies are Momo, about forty-five years old, so called from a wound in his face or cheek, from a ball, that disfigured him; (Wiskin), Cut-hair; (Washikick), Gourd rattle, (with whom I have had an interview;) (Oupichi), Big Man of the Sho-sho-ko. Augastasipa is the most noted. Both bands number probably over one thousand lodges of four persons each; of the relative portion of each band no definite account can be given; for, so soon as a Sho-sho-nie becomes too poor to, or does not, own a horse, he is called a Sho-sho-ko; but as soon as a Sho-sho-ko can, or does, own a horse, he is again a riding Indian, and therefore a Sho-sho-nie.

The Mormon settlements in the Salt Lake valley has not only greatly diminished their formerly very great resource of obtaining fish out of Utah Lake and its sources, which to them was an important resource; but their settlement, with the great emigration there, and to California, has already nearly driven away all the game, and will unquestionably deprive them almost entirely of the only chances they have for food. This will, in a few years, produce a result not only disastrous to them, but must inevitably engage the sympathies of the nation. How is this to be avoided, is a question of much difficulty; but it is, nevertheless, the more imperative on the Government, not only to discuss, but to put in practice, some mode of relief for those unfortunate people.

Brigham Young designated the Valley of the Great Salt Lake as the State of Deseret. In a short time, (1849) it became advisable for the settlers to establish, for the benefit of all, some judicial authority that could not be questioned by anyone in the area, whether a member of the Church or not, and this authority must be recognized by the United States. Further, the Mormons felt that if they neglected to establish such government, the incoming gentiles (derogatory name for non-Mormons), would do so.

The Utahs probably amount to from two to three thousand lodges and are divided into many bands – as to the Taos, three hundred lodges; Yam-pah-pa Utahs, five hundred lodges; Ewinte (Uinta), fifty lodges; Tenpenny Utahs (Timpanogos), fifty lodges; (these bands are about all who reside in the Salt Lake Valley), Pavant Utahs, not estimated; Pah or (pey) metes Utahs and the Sanpitch Utahs; of these last bands numbers are not known. Their claim of boundaries is south of that of the Shoshones, embracing the waters of the Colorado, going most probably to the Gulf of California. Their language is, suppose to, be substantially the same as that of the Sho-sho-nies; for although on the first meeting they do not fully understand each other, yet I am informed four or five-days association enables them to converse freely together. Some of these people are already engaged in the cultivation of the soil, and large tracts of the country afford ample rewards to those who thus expend the sweat of their brow. Portions of them are at present at variance with the Sho-sho-nies, and, indeed, the manners and customs of the Yam-pah-pah. Their country being more south and out of the range of white settlements or emigrants, the game is not likely to be as scarce for many years to come as it is in the Sho-sho-nie country even now, for already it has nearly all left their boundaries, except a small corner in the northeast corner of their claim; and, as they are at war with the Utahs, near whose lines it is, they are afraid to go there to hunt. I have concluded so to arrange matters before I leave, that both these nations will be able to send large delegations, if not most of the principal bands of their tribes, to a great council to be held here next summer, being not only by far the most convenient place for such a council, but is also where the principal agency ought to be established; and here, also, ought to be established the leading military post of these mountains, for which, hereafter, I shall give my views more at large. It is of great importance that these Utahs should be laid under obligations to cease their accustomed depredations on the whites and their property; and it is of greater importance to adopt some mode or other to save the Snakes from utter destitution, which in a year or two must inevitably take place, if things remain as they are now.

I write this in great haste; and the shortness of my stay here must be my excuse for not writing more, but I have touched on all the subjects most important at the present moment. When I get to Salt Lake, I shall have more time, and will go more into detail. Till then, I remain your obedient servant.[25]

---

25 Commissioner of Indian Affairs Annual Report 1849-1850. Letter dated August 22, 1849, from John Wilson to Honorable T. Ewing, Secretary of Department Interior.

CHAPTER 9:

1800's

In February 1848, with the Treaty of Guadalupe Hidalgo, the present states of California, Nevada, Arizona, Utah, and part of Montana were ceded to the United States by Mexico, as well as portions of Arizona, New Mexico, Colorado, and Wyoming. This cession, commonly referred to as the Mexican Cession of 1848, was a condition for the end of the Mexican American War. Once Utah became part of the United States, Mormons formed a theocratic political government; the People's Party, and petitioned Congress to designate the region they occupied as the State of Deseret. The State of Deseret encompassed the Great Basin, the Colorado River Basin, and a corridor to the Pacific Ocean around San Diego. However, the application for statehood was denied by the government of the United States because lawmakers were not inclined to grant the Mormons control over such a vast domain.

The United States began creating territories out of the newly acquired lands. Utah Territory was established in 1850, with Brigham

Young as Governor. The territory included all the present-day area of Utah, Nevada, western Colorado, and the extreme southwest corner of present-day Wyoming. In 1851, Brigham Young was informed that Congress was extending the Intercourse Act over Utah and that he was appointed Superintendent of Indian Affairs. The act made provisions for an Indian Agent and as many sub-agents as needed.

By proclamation, the first Governor of Utah Territory, Brigham Young, divided the territory into three agencies: the Parvan, Uinta, and Parowan. The 'Parvan' Agency included all those Indians that lay within the limits of the territory north of the Parvan Valley and west of the Shoshones. The 'Uinta' Agency included the Yuta and Shoshones; Ewintes or Uintas, Pah-Vant, San-Pitch, Tim-pa-noys, Cummum-bah, Tumpanawach, Uinta-At 'Yutas', and the Yampah Utah (not to be confused with the Colorado Uintah Yampa) and other fragments of Shoshone Indian bands and family clans in Utah Territory. The 'Parowan' Agency included all the country lying west of the Eastern Rim of the Great Basin, across the floor of the Salt Lake Valley, and south of the south line of the Parvan Valley, to the western boundary of the territory of Nevada.

In 1850 Governor Brigham Young issued an order to exterminate the Timpanogos Shoshone Indians living in the Utah Valley. The Mormon militia visited their encampment in friendship, then proceeded to line them up and execute them. Dozens of Timpanogos women and children were enslaved. The Mormons wanted the lands surrounding Utah Lake and decided that genocide was the most expedient method to get them. By 1870 the Federal Government determined that the Timpanogos Tribe no longer existed, if there were any survivors, they had been absorbed by the other bands and still others eventually had migrated to the Uinta Valley Reservation in northeastern Utah Territory.

These Native people were pushed south within said Utah Territory and east of the eastern rim of the Great Basin in what is now the landed area located in the east and northeastern half of the State of Utah that includes the Ashley Valley where the Shoshone Uinta-ats have lived even before the 1100's, within the Uinta River Basin that adjoins the western border of the State of Colorado and runs 60 miles inward to the banks of the Green River. A large portion of this designation was set apart by Presidential order as the Uinta River Valley Reservation in 1861. Commissioner Reports and documents identify the Uintas as Shoshone or Yuta Indians regardless that the natives at the Uinta Agency are not ethnically identified after 1861 as Yuta-Shoshone Indians but just as the "Uinta Band". The "extermination order" was an order issued by Brigham Young through Daniel H. Wells, on January 31, 1850, to stop "the operations of all hostile Indians and otherwise act as the circumstances may require, exterminating such, as do not separate themselves from their hostile Clans, and sue for peace."[26]

Mormons were not above using violence as a means of accomplishing their goals and this is true of Brigham Young's instructions in some cases, particularly concerning the Mormon attack on Black Elk and Patsowet's Tumpanawach (Timpanogas) Utahs near Utah Lake in 1850.

Mormons acquired some children and women as prisoners in the wake of attacks on Indian villages.

---

26 Brigham Young at a council meeting on January 31, 1850.

On January 31, 1850, Isaac Higbee, Bishop of Fort Utah, met with Governor Brigham Young, militia leader General Daniel H. Wells, the First Presidency, and the Quorum of the Twelve Apostles to petition Young for a war order. He stated, "that all the occupants of Fort Utah, who were in agreement, that they should go to war." Parley P. Pratt and Willard Richards argued for the killing of the Timpanogos. Brigham Young ordered an extermination campaign against them, with orders to kill all the men, but save the women and children who behaved. General Wells drafted the extermination order as Special-Order No. 2 and sent them to Captain George D. Grant. In his letter, he told Grant "Take no hostile Indians as prisoners" and "let no escape but do the work up clean". The Nauvoo Legion was sent from Salt Lake City and on February 8, 1850, they attacked the Timpanogos village. Their initial strategy was to encircle them and kill all hostile Timpanogos. The next day, the Timpanogos suffered many casualties and Chief Opecarry was wounded. Joseph Higbee, son of Isaac Higbee, was the only casualty of the Mormons. The Timpanogos fled during the night after the second day of fighting. They split into two groups. Pareyarts took a small group of wounded and sick and fled to Rock Canyon. Opecarry took the rest of the Timpanogos towards the Spanish Fork River.[27]

One contingent, under Captain Grant's command, followed the trail of Pareyarts into the canyon, killing more Timpanogos and taking prisoners. Some of the prisoners were later executed. The other contingent, led by Wells, divided into smaller parties, and searched the southern valley for Timpanogos to kill. They first attacked a village along the Spanish Fork River, and then a village on Peteetneet Creek. On February 13, 15–20 Timpanogos families surrendered to Captain

---

27 (Jared Farmer, On Zion's Mount: Mormons, Indians, and the American Landscape, (Cambridge, MA: Harvard University Press, 2008.)

Grant in modern-day Lake Shore, Utah. On February 14, Brigham Young wrote a letter instructing Wells to kill them if they did not surrender. Lieutenant Gunnison of the Stansbury Expedition reported that the Mormons promised to be friendly to the Timpanogos men. They held them prisoner overnight; but then in the morning lined up the Timpanogos men to be executed in front of their families. Some attempted to flee across the frozen lake, but the Mormons ran after them on horseback and shot them. Later in the day on February 14, the Nauvoo Legion spotted five more Timpanogos men on horseback, and killed three of them. On February 15, they killed three more men on the Peteetneet River. A government surgeon, James Blake, went to the execution site and cut off the Timpanogos' heads for later examination. Captain Howard Stansbury wanted the heads for "future scientific study" and planned to take them to Washington. Around 50 decapitated Timpanogos heads were gathered. They were supposed to be shipped to Salt Lake, but they were held up to be displayed in front of the prisoners at Fort Utah as a warning. More than forty prisoners, mostly women and children, were taken and placed with Mormon families "as servants" in Salt Lake City "for the purpose of weaning them from their savage pursuits and bringing them up in the habits of civilized and Christian life". It did not go as planned, as many died and most escaped to live with other Utah bands. News of the enslavement reached the U.S. Government and became one of the first priorities of Edward Cooper after he was appointed as Indian Agent of Utah later that year.[28]

The settlers in Utah then made a law to keep all Indians out of the fort. Pareyarts, who was sick with the measles, came in for some medicine and went to Sister Hunt's house; where Alexander Williams

---

28 Howard A. Christy, Utah Historical Quarterly Volume XLVI Open Hand and Mailed Fist: Mormon-Indian Relations in Utah, 1847–52) (S JH, January 31, 1850; HBY, 1850:17–18. "Statement made by Elder James Bean (June 12, 1854).

saw him and took him by the nape, and kicked him out of the fort. That same evening the Indians stole three cows out of Mrs. Hunt's yard and continued stealing, which was the commencement of Indian difficulties.

However, Utah was organized as a territory of the United States on September 9, 1850, under an Organic Act of Congress. The Compromise of 1850 attempted to resolve the territorial and slavery controversies caused by the Mexican American War by admitting California into the Union as a free state and creating the territories of Utah and New Mexico. For a time, it stretched from California to the Continental Divide, including all of what is now Utah together with large parts of Nevada, Colorado, and southwestern Wyoming. Mormon President, Brigham Young, was appointed governor of the new territory. Several times during the 1850s, non-Mormon officials appointed to govern Utah Territory served briefly, resigned their posts, and returned to Washington. They reported that Young and his ruling council obstructed them in their duties, sometimes with threats of violence or by ordering actual assaults.[29]

Brigham Young sent the Mormon militia to the Fort in 1853. Bridger learned they were coming and fled before the Mormons arrived. Later that year, the Mormons established Fort Supply about twelve miles south of Fort Bridger, spec Bridger complained to Gen. B. F. Butler, a U.S Senator, claiming the Mormons had robbed him of over $100,000 in goods and supplies and threatened him with death. The next spring, Young sent a detachment of well-armed Mormons to take control of both Fort Bridger and the Green River ferries, both of which became integral parts of the Mormon settlement plans for the region. The Mormons built a large stone wall around the fort.

---

29 Andrés Reséndez. The Other Slavery: The Uncovered Story of Indian Enslavement in America. Hubert Howe Bancroft. History of Utah, 1540-1886

The Battle at Fort Utah (also known as Fort Utah War or Provo War) was a battle between the Timpanogos Tribe and remnants of the Nauvoo Legion (a Mormon militia) at Fort Utah in modern-day Provo, Utah. The Timpanogos people initially tolerated the presence of the settlers, and the two groups enjoyed some moments of mutual friendship. However, after three Mormons murdered a Timpanogos man called Old Bishop and endured a hard winter where Timpanogos took around 50 Mormon cattle, settlers in Fort Utah petitioned to go to war with the Timpanogos. Isaac Higbee, Parley P. Pratt, and Willard Richards convinced Brigham Young to exterminate any Timpanogos hostile to the Mormon settlement. Young sent the Nauvoo Legion down with Captain George D. Grant and later sent General Daniel H. Wells to lead the army.

After the Timpanogos defended themselves, they fled from their camp to an abandoned cabin. The Mormons pursued them and any other Timpanogos they found in the valley, killing those from Chief Pareyarts or Para-yah (Old Elk) tribe and other tribes even if they had no history of attacking the Mormons. The Nauvoo Legion killed around 100 Timpanogos in that siege.[30]

The Deseret News (Salt Lake City, Utah)
26 JULY 1851

PROCLAMATION, To All whom it may Concern. Whereas, the law of Congress, entitled "An Act to establish a Territorial Government for Utah, approved September 9, 1850, involves the duties of Superintendent of Indian Affairs within said Territory, upon the Governor of said Territory; and, Whereas, there have been appointed by the United States

---

30 Historian's Office general Church minutes 1839-1877; 1846-1850; 1850 January-March; Salt Lake City; LDS Church History Library.

Government one Indian Agent, and two Sub-Agents for the Territory: Now, therefore by virtue of said authority, and to advance the purposes of the Government, for the benefit of the Indians, I do hereby order and direct that this Territory be divided into three Agencies as follows: to wit – The first, or 'Parvan' Indian Agency, to include all within the limits of the Territory, west of the Shoshone nation, and north of the south line of the Parvan Valley. The second, or 'Uinta' Agency, to include all the Yuta or Shoshones within the Territory; the Uinta and Yampa, & all other tribes, south, within said territory, and east of the eastern rim of the Great Basin. The third, or 'Parowan' Agency, to include all the country lying west of the eastern rim of the Great Basin, and south of the south line of the Parvan Valley, to the western bounds of the Territory.

Henry R. Day and Stephen B. Rose, the Sub-Agents having arrived, and being ready to enter upon the discharge of their respective duties, are hereby temporarily, and until further directions, assigned to their respective agencies, as follows: to wit – Henry R. Day to the first or 'Parvan' agency; and Stephen B. Rose to the second, or 'Uinta' agency.[31]

In a letter dated September 29, 1852, Brigham Young reported a peace talk which was held in Salt Lake City between the Utahs (Yutas) and Shoshones. Chief Wachor (Wakara) representing the Utahs and Chief Wash-o-kig (Washakie) representing the Shoshones. Both parties wished to make peace and be friends with each other.

On the 6th day of August, there arrived in this city six of the Shoshonee, as messengers from that tribe to make inquiry in relation to trade, and to ascertain if possibly, peace might be made with Wachor (Wakara) and the Utahs. This being a desirable object to

---

31 Brigham Young, Governor of the Utah Territory, and Superintendent of Indian Affairs G.S.L. City, July 21, 1851.)

accomplish, I made the messengers some present, and informed them that I would send for the Utahs, to meet them, if they would come, and endeavor to accomplish the object which they seemed so ardently to desire. Accordingly, on the 3d of September, after many fruitless efforts on our part to procure the Utahs, who appeared very wary and inclined to try the patience of the Shoshones to the uttermost, they were brought together; the Shoshones having been in waiting some two or three weeks. There were present on the part of the Utahs, Wakara, Sow-e-ett, Antazo (Antero), Ankar-howhitch (Arrow-pine being sick), and dirt-floor lodges; on the part of the Shoshones, Washakie, To-ter-mitch, Watche-namp, Ter-ret-e-ma, Pershe-go, and twenty-six lodges.

The lodges were left a short distance from the city, the braves, amounting to about fifty in number on each side, attending the treaty. Both Wakara and Washakie wished for peace and spoke with their braves. They all agreed to peace, rose, and held up their right hand. I then told them that they must never fight each other again, but live in peace, so that they could travel in each other's country, and trade with each other. The pipe of peace, being first offered to the Great Spirit, was often replenished, and sent around by the Sho-shonie chiefs, until everyone had smoked in token of lasting friend-ship. The Utahs were then asked if they had any objections to our settling on their lands, and, if they had not, to raise their right hands, which they did unanimously. Sow-e-ette, being the chief of the Uinta Yutas (two of his sons being present) was also asked the same ques-tion. He replied that it was good for them to have us settle upon their lands, and that he wanted a house close beside us. I then asked the Shoshones how they would like to have us settle upon their lands at the Green River. They replied that the land at Green River did not belong to them; that they lived and inhabited in the vicinity of the Wind River chain of mountains and the Sweet River, (or Sugar Water, as they called it;), but that if we would make a settlement on the Green River, they would be glad to come and trade with us.

The Shoshones were expecting that Wakara and the Yutas (Utahs) would give them some horses, according to their usual custom, for a certain number of Shoshones which they had killed in their last conflict, which occurred something over a year ago. Ten seemed to be the number which had been killed, and the same number of horses were required, but finally agreed upon nine head. Wakara now led off in quite a lengthy speech, in which he said that he had done wrong, and was very sorry for it. His friends had been killed on the Shoshones' land, and he had supposed that they had done it; but now he was satisfied that it was not them.[32]

During 1853-54, there occurred what was known as the Wakara War. Wakara was a favorite chief of the 'Yutas' or Utahs. He had three well-known brothers: Arapeen, San-Pitch, and Tabby-To-Qwanah, and half-brothers; Grosepine, Ammon, Young Uinta, Battease, Tobiob (The Clouds), and Namutum Uinta. Wakara also had two sisters; Parumputs Jane Towats and Tahvap Dora Copperfield and one half-sister; Viroque Uinta. Wakara was in the prime of his life, in addition to several of the Native dialects he could converse fluently in Spanish and make himself understood in English. Before the coming of the Mormons, he made frequent raids into towns throughout New Mexico and California, looting taking captives for ransom, the slave trade, and stealing many horses. He was a wealthy man by Indian standards.

---

32 Commissioner of Indian Affairs Annual Report 1852 Utah Superintendency No. 63 from Brigham Young, Governor and ex-officio Superintendent of Indian Affairs, Utah Territory.

At first Wakara received the exiled saints, with open arms he gave them information as to the nature of the country, advised them where to establish settlements, and guarded them from depredation. But when he saw that they had occupied his choicest lands; when game disappeared from the canyons and mountain sides; and when his people were shot down without provocation, and their cattle stolen by bands of emigrants, his friendship turned to hostility and anger, and he longed to rid himself of the white man.

CHAPTER 10:

Indian Wars

Wakara War: Growing tension between the Mormon settlers and the Utah Indians resulted in the Walker War. The war was sparked on July 17, 1853, by a confrontation with James Anderson Ivie in Springville in Utah Valley. It resulted in the death of a band member, Shower-O-Cats, a relative of Wakara. The Indians wanted to trade goods near Ivie's home, when Ivie tried to intervene in an argument over a trade between a Utah and his wife. Ivie wounded several of the Indians and one died. When Ivie would not comply with Indian requests for compensation, believing that he acted in self-defense, tension between Mormon settlers and the Utahs reached its peak.

A Mormon militia unit went to Wakara's camp in Payson to work out a peaceful resolution; however, no arrangement was agreed upon. The Utahs demanded retribution, seeking the death of a Euro-American. When the Mormons refused, the Utah shot and killed Alexander Keele on July 18, 1853, in Payson. This event was the tipping point in the relations between the two groups. Indians started attacks in nearby towns. By July 25, Wakara was reported to be gathering Utahs for a war. Mormon colonels Peter Conover and Stephen Markham rounded up men and called for volunteers to pursue the Utah, and families were advised to fortify their houses, store their grains, and protect their livestock. In a defensive effort, Brigham Young directed settlers to move from outlying farms and ranches and establish centralized forts. His people began to heavily guard the travel routes between Mormon settlements.

Wakara and his warriors conducted raids against Mormon outposts in central and southern Utah; in turn Mormon militias retaliated. In one case four settlers driving oxen-drawn wagons to Salt Lake City from Manti were attacked and killed at Uintah Springs on the night of September 30, 1853. Historical accounts indicate that pioneers retaliated the next day, and intermittent fighting continued until early November. In December of that year, Young offered amnesty to all the Utah. They did not respond and continued to commit violent acts for several more weeks. On March 24, Young sent Major E.A. Bedell, the federal Indian agent, to meet with Wakara and other Utah leaders. Bedell was to inquire if they would make a treaty with Young for the sale of their land. During the meeting with Bedell, Wakara said that "he would prefer not to sell if he could live peacefully with the white people which he was anxious to do."

The Walker War ended through this understanding personally negotiated between Young and Wakara that was finalized in May 1854 in Levan near Nephi, Utah. In his contemporary work *Incidents of Travel and Adventure in the Far West* (1857), photographer and artist Solomon N. Carvalho gives an account of the peace council held between Wakara, other native leaders in central Utah, and Brigham Young. Carvalho took the opportunity to persuade the Indian leader to pose for a portrait, now held by the Thomas Gilcrease Institute, Tulsa, Oklahoma. Although immediate hostilities ended, none of the underlying conflicts were resolved. Wakara died after a lingering illness, possibly pneumonia, on January 28, 1855, while at Meadow Creek, Utah Territory.

On the 7th day of August 1855, a treaty was negotiated by the Indian Agent with the Shoshones and Utahs, whereby, for a consideration of $3,000 dollars, peace and friendship were to be confirmed with the United States, and the passage of United States citizens through their territory without molestation was to be guaranteed. The treaty was not ratified, and only a copy of it was received at Washington. On the 7th instant I had the gratification of meeting large bands of Shoshones (Snakes) and (Utahs) in council in this city, where they made a "good peace", which I hope will prove lasting.[33]

The Utah Lake and Provo River at this season of the year abound in fish, known as mountain trout, and it is for the purpose of fishing that so large several the tribe of Yuta or Utah Indians resort hither every spring. At the commencement the Indian manifested a very bad feeling towards the settlers, and I have no doubt, had not some measures of a specific nature been taken, that we would have a renewal of the difficulties which characterized the year 1853. Those first disposed for peace, were Tabba (Tabby-To-Kwanah), Sanpitch and Grosepine; the principal leaders of the disaffected were Tintick, Squash, and Autan-quer (Black Hawk). The principal chiefs of the Utahs are now on a visit to the Navajoes.[34]

---

33 Commissioner of Indian Affairs Annual Report 1855 No. 99 from Brigham Young, Governor and ex-officio Superintendent of Indian Affairs, Utah Territory.

34 Commissioners of Indian Affairs Report, No. 101, 1855 George W. Armstrong, Indian Sub-Agent, Utah Territory to His Excellency Governor Brigham Young, Ex-officio Superintendent Indian Affairs.

The Deseret News (SLC)
27 JUNE 1855

Home Correspondence – June 12, 1855, I fell in company with Elder Dimick B. Huntington – Utah and Shoshone interpreter, who was sent by the Superintendent of Indian Affairs to settle a difficulty between the Utahs and the inhabitants of Provo. On Friday, Mr. Huntington, and Major G.W. Armstrong, the Indian Sub-Agent, visited the Indians, who were camped in the Old Fort Field. The Indians had been requiring the people to throw open the Old Fort field and 400 acres of grass land adjoining, for their horses to feed, and had prohibited the people from fishing in the Provo River. Elder Huntington succeeded in pacifying the Indians, and getting them to move out of the field, by the Agent engaging to fence in a pasture on the lower part of the Fort field, and to open a road on the banks of then Provo, from the city to said pasture, by the time the Indians want to come again to fish. The principal leaders of the disaffected were Tintick, Squash, and An-ton-guer; and those who were first disposed for peace were Tabby, Sanpitch, and Grosepine. Mr. Armstrong gave them horses, and a yearling steer to pay-for a mare and colt that they charge to the whites as having killed, although there is no evidence to that effect, neither is it believed that the whites have interfered with those animals. Tintick was very mad at first, but after a long conversation he became quiet. Mr. Huntington inquired what he was mad about; he replied he was mad because he had been told that Brigham had ordered Tabby to come and arrest him: he was told that if he did not stop committing depredations upon the whites he would be arrested, and if he was mad at that, he might say so. The interpreter requested one of the Indians to fill the pipe of peace, and pass it around, when Tintick burst out into a loud laugh, and said: "I see I cannot scare you," and he came into the lodge, appeared friendly, and willingly agreed to the resolution of the others. The course pursued by

Major Armstrong with the Indians is highly satisfactory to the people of Provo, and the citizens of Utah County generally. George A. Smith

The Deseret News (SLC)
8 AUGUST 1855

Our Correspondence – The Indians in Utah County; Editor of the Deseret News: I left the city on Thursday, July 12, and arrived in Springville at 7:30 p.m. On the next morning, Friday 13, Tin-tic, one of the head ones of that band, paid me a visit. He was very cold and indifferent at first, but after my talking to him some time, he got warmed up, and said he felt better. I told him I wanted to see all, of the band and talk with them, and that I had a letter from the agent for them. The message was circulated, and I was surrounded by about 50, among whom were Tab-by, Ton-om-bu-gah, Sanpitch, and other principal head men. After smoking the pipe of peace, I spoke to them about three quarters of an hour upon the subject of the whites living on their land, and of their becoming civilized. The head men replied that they wanted the whites to live here, and live in peace, for it was bad to fight and spill blood upon the ground. They said that they knew very well that some of their unruly boys would stop up their ears, so that they could not hear, and they believed that some of the whites also stopped their ears. After talking with them three and a half hours, I gave them some tobacco. They said that before I came, they had lost the Good Spirit, but after hearing me talk, they said that their ears were now open, and they went away feeling first rate.

Sunday 15th, I called upon all the Indians at Springville to go with me to see the Big Cap-i-tan at Provo; they readily consented, and about 50 of them rode in double file, by order of one of the chiefs. At the bowery the Indians were all seated, so that they could hear all that was said. After a lengthy discourse from His Excellency the Governor,

Brigham Young, I was called to the stand, together with the chiefs, to address the congregation. Ton-om-bugah spoke a short time, and I interpreted. I also made a brief statement of what the Governor had said. They said that their hearts felt good and went away well satisfied. On the 7th instant I had the gratification of meeting large bands of Shoshonees (Snakes) and (Utahs) in council in this city, where they made a "good peace" which I hope will prove lasting.[35]

We returned to this city on the 22d day of August, and, as you are aware, were visited on the 24th by a band of Shoshones, or Snakes proper, under a chief by the name of Ti-ba-bo-en-dwart-sa, (white man's friend,) numbering in all, about three hundred, who had come to this place, according to previous arrangements with the Utahs, for the purpose of holding a treaty with them. In a few days they were joined by the Utahs and Cum-mum-bahs, making it all, about five hundred souls. It was well understood among the Indians of this Territory, as early as last spring, that large appropriations had been made by Congress for the purpose of making presents to, and treaties with them. The season was passing away and the Indians were anxious to know why these presents did not come. The Snakes complained that they had permitted the white people to make roads through all their lands and travel upon them in safety, use the grass and drink the water, and had never received anything for it, all though the tribes around them had been getting presents.

Early last spring I was induced to think that some of the Utahs and Pah-Vants could be taught to farm and to appreciate the advantages of agriculture. I, therefor, had land marked off for them, and designated suitable persons to instruct them how to work. Many

---

35 Commissioner of Indian Affairs Annual Report 1855 No. 99 from Brigham Young, Governor and ex-officio Superintendent of Indian Affairs to Hon. George W. Manypenny, Commissioner of Indian Affairs, Washington City, D.C.

of them are destitute of anything to subsist upon, and hunger had forced them to leave the farm and go to the mountains to hunt, or to the creeks to fish. Owing to the great blight, in consequence of the grasshoppers, our farms have produced but little to show, for the amount, of labor bestowed upon them. I would take occasion to suggest here that treaties ought to be negotiated with these tribes, as early as possible, for the title to their lands, which are now held and occupied by the whites. It is a thing almost unprecedented in the history of our Indian policy to go into any State or Territory and make extensive and permanent improvements upon soil claimed by Indians without extinguishing those claims by treaty.

This delay is not only unjust to the Indian, by depriving them of their wanted hunting grounds, without paying that respect to their claims which is due them, according to our usage with other tribes, but it is equally so to the pioneer settler, who is forced to pay a constant tribute to these worthless creatures, because they claim that the land, the wood, the water, and the grass are theirs, and we have not paid them for these things.[36]

A report was circulated that a mare and colt had been killed, belonging to a chief of the Utah tribe of Indians, named Tintick. Immediately after my return, I commenced an investigation of the matter, I proceeded with my interpreter to the Indian camp, consisting of forty lodges, which they had located in a well enclosed field, containing some four hundred acres of grain and grass. I held a talk with Tintick, and Tabby and Sanpitch, who are chiefs of the same tribe. I learned from them that the report was correct, and that they charged the commission of the deed upon a white man named

---

36 Commissioner of Indian Affairs Annual Report 1855 No.100 from Garland Hurt, Indian Agent for Utah to His Excellency Brigham Young, Governor and Ex-Officio Superintendent Indian Affairs, Utah Territory.

Chester Snyder. Tintick was very "mad," and complained much at the loss of his animals and demanded pay of me as remuneration for the same, and I soon learned that the same bad feeling reigned throughout the entire camp. As soon as circumstances would admit, I had an interview with Snyder, and informed him of the charge preferred against him by the chief. Snyder protested his innocence and satisfied me by the most convincing proof that he was innocent, as he was at the time absent from the city when the animals were killed; and furthermore, none of the Indians could identify Snyder as the man who committed the act. That the animals were dead admits of no doubt, as Tintick took me to the place where the animals were, and I saw for myself. I told the chiefs that I would endeavor to discover who killed the animals, and have the individual punished, and him paid. Before I succeeded in settling the difficulty, there were killed five head of cattle and one horse, belonging to the citizens of this city, which I have reason to believe was done by the Indians. They had also turned their horses into fields, destroying a large amount of grain which had hitherto escaped the ravages of grasshoppers. I demonstrated with them on the course they were pursuing and informed the chiefs that unless their men would cease their depredations, I would not pay for the animals which they had lost and would most assuredly punish the offenders. They then agreed, if I would pay for the animals, that they would immediately move their camp out of the enclosed fields and would not encroach upon the property of the settlers for the future. I accordingly paid them, which will be seen by reference to voucher No. 6, and they left the field forthwith, and peace was restored.

The chiefs complained to me that they could not catch their usual supply of fish, in consequence of some of the citizens using nets to their disadvantage. I immediately issued notices to the companies then fishing in Utah Lake and Provo River to cease their operations during the stay of the Indians, which was immediately complied with. The Indians then attempted to take fish in their usual way, that of trapping, shooting with bow and arrows, etc., but, in consequence of the high stage of the water in the river, which always occurs at this season of the year, they were enabled to catch but very few. At the instance of some of the chiefs I requested one of the fishing companies to fish for them, which request the company immediately complied with, and, after some days successful fishing, they loaded the pack horses of the Indians with a large quantity of fish. The Utah Lake and Provo River at this season of the year abound in fish known as mountain trout. It is for the purpose of fishing that several of the tribe of Utah Indians resort hither every spring. They requested that a pasture should be made for them bordering on the Provo River near their fishing grounds, where they could fish, at the same time protect themselves and animals from the Shoshone, or Snake Indians. It is of great importance that these Utahs should be laid under obligations to cease their accustomed depredations on the whites and their property.

Those first deposed for peace were Tabby, Sanpitch, and Grosepine; the principal leaders of the disaffected were Tintick, Squash, and Autan-quer (Blackhawk) The principal chiefs of the Utahs are now on a visit to the Navajoes. They informed me that they would return about the first of September, when the matter will be finally determined upon.[37]

Since my last report, dated August 14, which closed my official duties as sub-agent, I was informed that Sawriet (Sow-e-ette) had returned on a visit to this place after an absence of two years.

---

37 Commissioner of Indian Affairs Annual Report 1855 No.101 from John Wilson to Secretary of the Department.

On the 22d of August last, I received a visit from seventeen of his chiefs and braves, who informed me that the citizens of Palmyra (Spanish Fork) told them that I was an agent of the government of the United States, and that they had a great desire to see me and have a talk. Anthers-be-a-ho-a, "big chief" and one of the deputations, acted as spokesman on the occasion. He informed me of the object of their visit by stating that in the vicinity of Santa Fe they were told by a Delaware Indian and an emigrant that the "big chief at Washington" (meaning the President) had sent the Utah Indians, a large amount of presents and that they had come to receive their portion. He expressed considerable surprise and regret when I told him he had been misinformed, and that no presents had arrived, and that he must not believe any more reports of a similar kind, until he received the intelligence from some of the authorized agents of the government of the United States. I was informed that in so many sleeps (about three weeks) the old chief himself would visit me and have a talk; that he was very old (about seventy-five) and tired of riding, that he would have to rest himself before he could see me. After the council ended the party took a tour of the city of Provo, once done they returned to Palmyra (formerly Spanish Fork), where the old chief was encamped. This band, numbering seventy lodges, are the most harmless and friendly of any of the Yuta Indians. About the beginning of the Indian war of 1853, this band would not take part against the whites, and quietly left the scene of action, and have not since returned until the present. About the eighth of this month, I was visited by the old chief in person, who was friendly, together with Roo-ea-gwosh (or Horse Tail), Tshare-puegin (or White-eye), who made about the same statements as the others. The old chief expressed the same disappointment and regret, saying that he had rode a great distance to receive his presents, but said he had been misinformed and that he would not complain. He asked me if I would not give him some presents, and his band something to eat. I arrived at Springville on Monday but, much to my surprise, he and his band had left for Winta (Uinta) Valley.[38]

In January of this same year, Chief Wakara died and the leading spirit of the 'Yutas' let their midst. He was succeeded by his brother Arapeen; Arapeen was succeeded by San-Pitch, and Tabby-To-Qwanah succeeded San-Pitch and was afterward chief of the 'Yutas' or Utahs. It was Chief Tabby who led his people, headed by several sub-chiefs, to the Uinta River Valley Basin Reservation in northeastern Utah after it was set apart from the public domain by Executive Order 38-1 by the United States President for the 'Yuta' or 'Utah' Shoshone Indians in 1861.

The Mormons controlled the Fort Bridger for a year, until July 1855, when Jim Bridger returned. They asked him to sell but, seeing the new improvements, Bridger balked. After several months, he finally agreed. But the tensions for the Mormons were far from over and followed years of tension between the Mormons and the federal government over questions of sovereignty, polygamy, land rights, water rights and the authority of courts. The U.S. Army, under the command of Col. Albert Sidney Johnston, planned to use Fort Bridger as a base of operations for the march into Utah. But, before they could seize the fort, Mormon militia under "Wild Bill" Hickman and his brother burned it and Fort Supply. As a result, Johnston's army spent a miserable winter with little shelter and food.

Throughout this period of territorial development in the western United States, Mormon leaders made additional attempts to gain

---

38 Commissioner of Indian Affairs Annual Report 1855 No. 102 from George W. Armstrong, Indian Agent to His Excellency Brigham Young, Ex Officio Superintendent of Indian Affair.)

statehood, as statehood was considered integral to independence in local affairs. In 1856, Mormons sent Congress a draft of a constitution for a state much smaller than the proposed State of Deseret. Simultaneously, the Republican Party's first presidential campaign was featuring a platform that denounced slavery and polygamy. This denouncement produced friction between the federal government and the Mormons, and eventually resulted in the Utah War (1857-1858).

Prior to my report of December 31,1855, it became evident that our relations with the Utahs were of the most delicate character; and but for the timely intervention of propositions which I made for designating certain tracts of land for their future permanent homes, and to assist them in opening the farms and putting in crops, there was scarcely a doubt that a general state of hostilities would have been commenced before this time. But, without authority from government for making permanent arrangements of this kind, and without funds to meet expenditures thus incurred, the adoption of such a course was, to say the least of it, assuming high responsibilities. But the only apology I shall offer is, that the circumstances left me without an alternative. The friendly bands of Utahs mentioned in my report of the 31st of March last have remained true to their pledge made me at that time and have kept aloof from Tintick's hostile band.[39]

Utah Territory, Office Superintendent (Great Salt Lake City)
30 JUNE 1856

In this connection, it may not be amiss for me to state that nearly two years have elapsed since Congress appropriated over forty thousand dollars for the express purpose of making treaties, etc.,** with the

---

39 Commissioner of Indian Affairs Report 1856 No. 99 from George w. Armstrong, Indian Agent

Indians in Utah, that their lands have been traversed by government surveying parties now almost a year, and still not one dollar of that appropriation has yet been expended within this superintendency, and, for aught I know, is still fast in the coffers at Washington. Is this just? Has it any precedent in usage toward tribes in any other State or Territory? More especially when the relative conduct, facilities, and advantages of the various tribes are taken into account.[40]

**Governor Young is mistaken in this, as the records of the Indian Office show that drafts to the amount of $27,074.80, drawn by himself and Agents Hurt and Armstrong, have been paid out of this appropriation for Indian purposes in Utah.

Superintendent Indian Affairs to Hon. George W. Manypenny, Commissioner Indian Affairs (Washington City, D.C.), Office Indian Agent (Great Salt Lake City, U.T.)

SEPTEMBER 1856

The friendly bands of Utahs mentioned in my report of the 31st of March last, have remained true to their pledge made me at the time, and have kept aloof from Tintick's hostile band. Of Tintick's band, but little is known. I learned from some of the friendly Indians that he was camped on West Mountain and had fortified himself at that point; but has since left and moved his camp to the Navajo country.[41]

Tintic War: The Tintic War was a short series of skirmishes occurring in February 1856 in the Tintic and Cedar Valleys of Utah, occurring after the conclusion of the Wakara War. It was named after a subchief

---

40 Commissioner Of Indian Affairs Report 1856 No. 97 from Brigham Young, Governor, and ex-officio Superintendent Indian Affairs

41 Commissioner of Indian Affairs Annual Report 1856 No. 99 from George W. Armstrong, Indian Agent to His Excellency Brigham Young, Ex Officio Superintendent of Indian Affairs.

of the Utah and involved several clashes between settlers and natives, mostly over the natives' theft of cattle because of drought. Originally the settlers and Indians got along fairly well. The war started out as small skirmishes between the settlers and Indians. Then the first battle occurred at Battle Creek. These occurred because the Indians had been displaced from their land by the settlers. During the winter they did not have the necessary resources to survive, and they started to starve. The Euro Americans invaded the area and proceeded to establish mining communities. They depleted the land of timber, game, diverted the water, and most of the land's resources in general.

The settlers did, however, establish successful livestock and agriculture endeavors on the land. The Indians were forced to start stealing from the settlers, to survive. Brigham Young was one of the settlers, and he recounts the early troubles by stating, "They came pretty nigh starving to death last winter; and they now see, if they are driven from these valleys in winter, they must perish". The war concluded with the federal government intervening. They took the Yutas from their land in the Salt Lake Valley to the Uinta Valley Reservation. This occurred in the late 1860s and in the Uinta Basin. However, the issues did not resolve overnight. The government never actually bought the Yuta lands. This caused issues that persisted after World War II. Then the Indian Claims Commission requested money for their confiscated lands.

Black Hawk War: From 1865 to 1867, "Antonga", called Black Hawk by the white settlers, led a force of warriors into an estimated 150 battles, skirmishes, raids, and military engagements on the Mormon settlements in Sanpete County, Sevier County, and other parts of central and southern Utah. The conflict resulted in the abandonment of some settlements and hindered Mormon expansion in the region. The war was not started by one singular event, but by a series of events. Unable to distinguish differences between tribesmen, frustrated Mormons indiscriminately killed Indians, including women and children".[42]

The Timpanogos bands of Utahs had been pushed aside by settlers' demands for grazing land and farmland. Frustrations on both sides led to several short battles. After the 'Battle of Fort Utah' in 1850, the 'Wakara War' in 1853-1854, and the 'Tintic War' in 1856, Mormon leaders persuaded the Utah leaders to stop hostilities when the losses incurred by Utahs were compensated with food, presents, and promises of future friendship. The white man, not knowing, or caring, was doing the same thing that other Indian tribes had faced everywhere white men settled. Indian removal was not a stated policy in Utah Territory until the elimination of the Indian farms at Spanish Fork and Twelve Mile Creek in the 1860's. Nevertheless, the practice of pushing the Indians into isolated and remote areas was a de facto removal policy. The white settlers saw good land, they perceived, going to waste, and were determined to utilize it. One attempt to upgrade the Indian was that of the Indian farm. Following the council of Governor Young, the five small reservations established in the counties of Utah, Juab, Sanpete, Millard, and Iron became known as Indian farms because some attempts were made to teach the Indians farming and ways of a sedentary life.

The Deseret News (Salt Lake City, Utah)
28 AUGUST 1867

Black Hawk – We had the pleasure of meeting Superintendent Head on Wednesday evening, who had arrived from Uinta Reservation, where

---

42 Josiah F. Gibbs, "Black Hawk's Last Raid," Utah Historical Quarterly, 4 October 1931.

he had met and had a talk with the notorious Black Hawk, who came there with his family, unattended by his warriors. Black Hawk said he has 28 lodges under his sole control; and that he is assisted by 3 Elk Mountain chiefs, who have each 10 or 12 lodges with them. These Indians are scattered along the settlements, he avers, from the north of Sanpete County to the southern settlements, watching opportunities to make raids. He expressed a desire for peace; said he could control and would be answerable for his band; and believed he could get the others with him, as they all looked to him as the head chief. He would try and get them all together at some point, perhaps Uinta, to have a talk with Colonel Head; but it would take some time to do this, as they are so scattered. As an earnest of his sincerity, he stated that he had made a covenant, when he commenced to fight, that he would not have his hair cut, and he talked strong of Tabby and Kan-osh who had theirs cut like white men; but now that he was going to have peace, he wished to have it cut, and requested the Superintendent to shorten his locks for him, which was done after finding that he was anxious to have it so. The savage was saucy at the opening of their interview, but finally toned down, and talked reasonable before they got through.

Black Hawk, the sub-chief who became the principal War Chief of the Utahs, was thought to be a Pah-Ute (Paiute – he was from the Utahs Tribe). He was born in the Southern part of Utah Valley, and as a youth played with the white children of the area. Black Hawk spoke English fluently due to his early association with the whites. His father was "Synnap Pich" (Sanpitch) or Tenaciono (something that hangs on). C. L. Christensen, an Indian interpreter, stated that Synnap Pich was a chief of the Sanpete area. His mother was Tanar-oh-wich (mother of boys). Black Hawk has been described as tall and stately. He supposedly had a long nose and looked as though he had a small mustache. He was intelligent and could make up his mind in a hurry. It was said that more than once, as a youth, he sat in Mormon meetings and listened to them plan defense against the Indians.[43]

Although Black Hawk made peace in 1867, other bands continued raiding. Black Hawk was suffering in the later stages of Tuberculosis, he left the Uinta Valley Reservation and returned to his home in Spring Lake, Utah. He died on September 27, 1870. In 1872 the U.S. Government intervened, with about 200 troops, ending the raiders skirmishes.

The names "Black Hawk" and "Antonga" by which he was known, are not "Ute" Indian names. "Black Hawk" was a name that Brigham Young, in jest, called the Yuta leader. Young's term became the name by which he is now commonly known. There were some three or more Indians the whites referred to as Black Hawk in Utah history. It is reminiscent of Chief Black Hawk of the Sauk and Fox Indian (Mesquaki) tribes and the Black Hawk War of 1832 in Illinois, where the Mormons had migrated from. To the Mexicans he was known as "Antonga".

---

43 Mary Goble Pay, Cited by Kate B. Carter, Our Pioneer Heritage Salt Lake City, Utah: Daughters of Utah Pioneers, 1966.

CHAPTER 11:

The Mormon War

New-York Tribune (New York, New York)
28 DECEMBER 1857

Later From 'The Mormon War': The Rebellion Fully Organized, Utah Declared Independent, Advance of the United States Army. From Our Special Correspondent – Camp in the South Pass October 22, 1857: The news received from Colonel Alexander's command to this date is that the intended march up Bear River to Soda Springs had been abandoned and that on October 18 it was moving toward Henry Fork, which flows into Green River south from Fort Bridger. In that vicinity I will wait for arrival of Colonel Johnston, Colonel Smith's battalion, the supply trains, and the dragoons. It is probable that a depot will be formed, in the neighborhood, of Fort Bridger (of which possession could readily be taken) from which future operations will be directed. At that date the assumption of the commander-in-chief by Colonel Johnston, and his arrival at Colonel Smith's camp, were not known to Colonel Alexander, but the express bearing the information reached him probably on the 9th. A party of Mormons, with which was Porter Rockwell – the same man who is accused of the attempt to assassinate Governor Boggs of Missouri – cut off 700 more head of cattle a few days before, directly from the rear of the Army. The Mormons have entrusted the commander-in-chief of their forces to Daniel H. Wells, whom they style Lieutenant-General. He dates his orders from Fort Bridger but in, reality posted with his forces on Bear River. I have heard no estimates of their strength. Two more prisoners were made by Colonel Alexander's command, on whose persons were found documents issued by Wells, enjoining them to retard the progress of the Army by burning grass, stealing cattle, destroying trains, or any other means short of taking life. One of them is named Taylor and the other Stowell. The two prisoners taken previously prove to be brothers of the notorious "Bill Hickman". The younger of them has been sent to Salt Lake City with a message or a letter, of the contents of which I am uninformed, the older being retained as surety for his return. A prisoner has also been made to-day in Colonel Smith's camp, who confesses that the Mormon band which burned the trains on Green River endeavored to employ him to steal cattle, etc. Brigham Young has sent a lengthy document to Colonel Alexander, covering several pages of foolscap paper, which seems to be a protest of his own attitude. No further account of its contents has reached us. An order was issued by Colonel Johnston several days since prohibiting any one from passengers reading any message across Green River westward without special authorization. The object, I presume, is to prevent the Mormons from gaining information of the movements of the supply trains and of the troops which will act as their escort, and to those conductors of trains which will act as their escort. To those conductors of trains who have entered bonds to deliver their goods in Salt Lake City before a certain date he has given official copies of this order, to insure them against responsibility for their detention. Mr. Irwin, for instance, the agent of Livingston, Kincaide & Co., sutlers (supplier) to the 24 Dragoons, has in his train goods which he is under bonds of $30,000 to deliver there before January 1, 1858. There is a Mormon train between us and Fort Laramie which is said to belong to the church and to be freighted with private property of Brigham Young. Colonel Johnston passed it at the beginning of this month, a day or two before he arrived at Laramie. It has been reported in Colonel Alexander's camp that Dr. Hurt, the United States Indian Agent, had been seized and hanged by the Mormons. He was almost the only exception in the general exodus of Government officials last spring, and remained at his post, on Spanish Fork, at the southern extremity of Lake Utah, about sixty miles from Salt Lake City. But Mr. Davidson a member of the firm of Perry & Co., sutlers (supplier) to the 10th Infantry, who returned to-day from a journey to Green River, where he had gone to purchase cattle, reports that he was stopped on his way by a Frenchman, who asked him to read a letter which he had been unable to understand on account of his imperfect knowledge of English. It proved to be a letter from Dr. Hurt, stating that he had escaped under the protection of a band of Utah Indians, and asking where he might find the troops. This letter the Frenchman said had been brought to him by a Utah Indian, who was present. Mr. Davidson, of course, sent directions by means of which the doctor can reach our camp, and he is expected to arrive daily. Three of the teamsters belonging to the supply trains which were burnt on the 5th were frozen to death in the storm on the 16th. They had traveled back to the South Pass with their fellow teamsters and after camping, on the night of the storm, they became intoxicated with whiskey, and wandered out in the snow.

The Daily Delta (New Orleans, LA)
22 DECEMBER 1857

Dr. Garland Hurt, the Indian Agent, and the only United States officer who remained in the Territory of Utah after the other officials left last spring, has affected his escape, and reached Colonel Johnston camp on the Sweetwater. Previous, to the departure of the other federal officers, Dr. Hurt had taken refuge with a band of Utah Indians, who were devoted to him; he was not in Salt Lake City when they left. Some twenty of these Indians guided him through the passes to the south of the Wintah (Uinta) Mountains. He was six weeks in reaching the South Pass.

On Dec. 30, 1857, Judge Eckels convened a grand jury that indicted Brigham Young, Daniel H. Wells, John Taylor, and "one thousand [other] persons and more" on four counts of treason. The case later failed on procedural grounds.

The Utah Expedition, commonly referred to as the 'Utah War', was an armed dispute guided by Jim Bridger, between Mormon settlers in the Utah Territory and United States Federal Government. The confrontation began in May 1857, when President Buchanan decided to send federal troops to Utah to ensure the successful installation of a new governor and a slate of territorial officers, including a chief justice and a superintendent of Indian affairs. Jim Bridger entered government service as a scout and guided numerous expeditions, Alfred Cumming was the newly appointed governor of Utah Territory, enroute with an Army escort to his new position. He and his wife Elizabeth had traveled from Fort Leavenworth in eastern Kansas Territory with a column of dragoons led by Lt. Col. Philip St. George Cooke. Cooke's unit was part of the Utah Expedition, a larger force of U.S. soldiers ordered to Utah Territory by President James

Buchanan more than five months earlier. The expedition's purpose was to escort Gov. Cumming and install and support him in his new position with military force if necessary.

In Utah, tensions had been rising all summer as reports and rumors trickled in from the East. Late in May, Utah Territory's delegate to Congress, John M. Bernheisel, a Mormon, had arrived in Salt Lake City, confirming what Young had already heard from his far-flung network of scouts and couriers: Buchanan planned to replace him. A month later, Young learned troops were mobilizing at Fort Leavenworth. Panic and fear spread throughout the territory. On September 11, 1857, at Mountain Meadows, 300 miles south of Salt Lake, militiamen of the Nauvoo Legion slaughtered 120 members of an Arkansas wagon train enroute to California.

Young and many of his followers believed that the Army's imminent attack was an apocalyptic event. On September 14 and 21, 1857 Young preached fiery sermons. Bishops and teachers went from house to house, chastising residents for their behavior and publishing the names and offenses of those who confessed. Most terrifying of all was the doctrine of "blood atonement," under which, for certain sins, only the loss of the blood and life of the sinner was sufficient sacrifice to save that person's soul.[44]

Near the end of May, Buchanan offered a pardon to the inhabitants of Utah Territory for their "seditions and treasons" if they agreed to obey the laws of the federal government. Brigham Young's response would determine whether Johnston and his men marched into Salt Lake Valley as occupiers or as helpers and protectors of loyal citizens. Young capitulated, at least outwardly. On June 26, Johnston

---

44 Phelps, Capt. John W. Diary. In MacKinnon, William P., ed. At Sword's Point, Part I: A Documentary History of the Utah War to 1858. Kingdom in the West, The Mormons and the American Frontier, vol. 10. Will Bagley, series editor. Norman, Okla.: Arthur H. Clark Company, 2008, 382.

and his troops entered Salt Lake City, largely deserted due to a prior order by Young, for his followers to move south. Still suspicious, the Mormons were prepared to burn the city as well as their homes farther south in the valley, and retreat to the mountains. This did not happen. Johnston established a camp about 40 miles south of Salt Lake City near present Fairfield, Utah. He named it Camp Floyd, in honor of the secretary of war. In addition to the 120 defenseless people killed at Mountain Meadows, seven other murders occurred in 1857 and 1858, in or near the Salt Lake Valley. Mormons were proven to have committed at least six; one man was beaten to death in his sleep while a prisoner of the Mormons. Systematic, thorough looting accompanied all 127 of these murders. When the Utah War ended in 1858, the U.S. government refused to honor either Bridger's or the Mormons' claim to the property.[45]

---

45 Hafen, LeRoy and Anne W. Hafen, eds. The Utah Expedition 1857-1858: A Documentary Account of the United States Military Movement under Colonel. Albert Sidney Johnston, and The Resistance by Brigham Young and the Mormon Nauvoo Legion. The Far West and the Rockies Historical Series 1820-1875, vol. 8. Glendale, Calif.: Arthur H. Clark Company, 1958.)

CHAPTER 12:

Imminent Danger

Tensions in Utah Territory had again escalated between the Mormons and other Americans, largely because of polygamy and the theocratic rule in Utah Territory by Brigham Young. The Utah War was an armed confrontation between Latter-Day Saint settlers (Mormons) in Utah Territory and the armed forces of the United States Government. Brigham Young's dream early-on, was to establish a State of Deseret in the territory then owned by Mexico. That dream ended with the Guadalupe Treaty. The confrontation lasted from May 1857 until July 1858; it was ended by President James Buchanan on the condition that they (Mormons) accept United States federal authority. As a result of the insurrection Brigham Young was replaced as governor of Utah Territory by Alfred Cumming. However, conflict between Mormons and the U.S. Government continued to escalate to the point that in 1890, Congress disincorporated the LDS Church, incorporated under the territorial government, and seized most of its assets. Soon thereafter, church president Wilford Woodruff issued a manifesto that officially suspended the practice of polygamy. It did not however, disavow or dissolve the existing plural marriage practices. Brigham Young's dream of a utopia is still trying to be realized. As a standard operating procedure (SOP), the followers of Mormonism move into key places inside a town or city government in a way one might not suspect, they penetrate and over-run local government and pack the government agencies with others of like-kind. Whereby, these human intermediaries take control of the administration and legislature of the town, city, or state government which appears to be common traits wherever they locate - even on Indian Reservations where the Natives soon became collateral damage.[46]

A company of emigrants from Arkansas, emigrating to California, arrived, and camped at a spring in the west end of Mountain Meadow Valley, on the 3d or 4th September 1857. On the 9th of said month, and near the said spring, one hundred and fifteen to one hundred twenty were inhumanly massacred.

The lives of seventeen children were spared, who were from two months to seven years old. This massacre was brought to my official notice by a letter from the Honorable C.E. Mix, received June 1858 instructing me to make inquiry, and recover, if possible, certain children, who it was supposed, were saved from the massacre, and were supposed to be living with Mormons and Indians. Sixteen of the surviving children were collected in July 1858 and were placed in a respectable family in Santa Clara, 350 miles south of this city, and were provided for by my directions. The seventeenth child was recovered last April. None of the children were claimed by or living among the Indians. They were taken from the field of slaughter

---

46 Gilbert King, The Aftermath of Mountain Meadows. The massacre almost brought the United States to war against the Church of Jesus Christ of Latter-day Saints, but only one man was brought to trial: John D. Lee, contributing writer in history for Smithsonian.com. February 29, 2012

the evening of the day their friends were killed, and conveyed in a wagon to Mr. Hamblin's house, in the east end of the valley, by John D. Lee and Daniel Tullis, and perhaps others. The following day the children were divided out and placed in different Mormon families, in Cedar City, Harmony, Santa Clara, etc., from whence they were collected, in pursuance of my directions. A massacre of such unparalleled magnitude, on American soil, must sooner or later demand thorough investigation. I have availed myself, during the last twelve months, of every opportunity to obtain reliable information about the said emigrant company, and the alleged causes of and circumstances which led to their treacherous sacrifice. Mormons have been accused of aiding the Indians in the commission of this crime. I commenced my inquiries without prejudice or selfish motive, and with a hope that, in the progress of my inquiries, facts would enable me to exculpate all white men from any participation in this tragedy and saddle the guilt exclusively upon the Indians; but, unfortunately, every step in my inquiries satisfied me that the Indians acted only a secondary part. Conflicting statements were made to me of the behavior of this emigrant company, while traveling through the Territory. I have accordingly deemed it a matter of material importance to make strict inquiry to obtain reliable information on this subject; not that bad conduct on their part could in any degree palliate the enormity of the crime or be regarded as any extension. My object was common justice to the surviving orphans. The result of my inquiries enables me to say that the company conducted themselves with propriety. They were camped several days at Corn Creek, Fillmore Valley, adjacent to one of our Indian Farms. Persons have informed me that, whilst there camped, they poisoned a large spring with arsenic, and the meat of a dead ox with strychnine. This ox died, unquestionably, from eating poisonous weed, which grows in most of the valleys here. Persons in the southern part of the Territory told me last spring, when on a southern trip, that from fifteen to twenty Pah-vant Indians (of those on Corn Creek farm) died from drinking the water of the poisoned spring and eating of the poisoned meat. Other equally unreasonable stories were told to me about these unfortunate people. That an emigrant company, as respectable as I believe this was, would carry along several pounds of arsenic and strychnine, apparently for no other purpose than to poison cattle and Indians, is too improbable to be true. I cannot learn that the Pah-vants had any difficulty with these people. The massacre took place only about one hundred miles south of Corn Creek, and yet not any of those Indians were present. Bad white men have magnified a natural cause to aid them in exciting the southern Indians, hoping that, by so doing, they could be relied upon to exterminate the said company and escape detection themselves. Thus, on the Monday morning, after, the Friday, 4th or 5th of September, the day they camped at the spring, the Indians commenced firing upon them, and continued daily until and during the eighth day of their encamping, but without accomplishing much. Several were killed, however, and a few wounded. When the company first apprehended an attack, they formed a corral with their wagons, and filled up with earth to the wagon-beds, which made a protective fort. White men were present and directed the Indians. John D. Lee, of Harmony, told me, in his own house, last April, in presence of two persons, that he was present three successive days during the fight, and was present during the fatal day. The Indians alone made their last attack on the 8th of September. On the 9th, John D. Lee, and others whose names I gave in my letter of the 23d ultimo, displayed a white flag, and approached the corral with two wagons, and had a long interview with the company, and proposed a compromise. What there occurred has not transpired. The emigrant company gave up all their arms, with the expectation that their lives would be spared and they would be conducted back to Panther Creek and Cedar City. The old women, children, and wounded, were taken in the wagons, and the company proceeded towards to Panther Creek, when suddenly, at a signal, the work of death commenced, about one and a half miles from the spring, at a place where there was about an acre of scrub-oak brush. Here not less, I think, than one hundred and fifteen men, women, and children, were slaughtered by white men and Indians. Three men got out of the valley, two of whom were soon overtaken and killed; the other reached Muddy Creek, over fifty miles off, and was overtaken and killed by several Indians and one white man.

Thus terminated the most extensive and atrocious massacre recorded in American History. Whoever may have been the perpetrators of this horrible deed, no doubt exists in my mind that they were influenced chiefly by a determination to acquire wealth by robbery. It is in evidence, from respectable sources, that material changes have taken place in the pecuniary condition of certain individuals suspected of complicity in this affair. It is to be regretted that no well-directed effort has been made to bring the guilty to trial and punishment. I furnished to the proper officials the names of some of the persons who, I had reason to suppose, were instigators and participators in this unparalleled massacre and with the names of witnesses. It was my intention to visit the southern portion of the Territory early last fall, for the purpose of bringing to this city the surviving children; but the public interest, the safety of the emigrants, and of the United States mail, then carried on the northern California road, required my presence among the Indians in the Humboldt Valley, which place I visited in September and October

1858. Upon my return from that region, the weather was too inclement to travel, with so many children, northwardly.

I started as early this spring as practicable and arrived back with the children the beginning of May. It is proper to remark, that when I obtained the children, they were in better condition than children generally in the settlements in which they lived.

In pursuance of instructions, I started fifteen of the surviving children the 29th of last June for Leavenworth City, under the general supervision of Major Whiting, United States Army, and special care of several females. When I leave for the States, under your authority, I will take with me the two boys, who, at the time of the massacre, were, respectively, six and seven years old, and who were detained here by the United States Attorney General in the hope that important facts of testimony might be elicited from them.

It is proper in connection with the foregoing, to state that this emigrant party, previous to, the massacre, was in possession of a large quantity of property, consisting of horses, mules, oxen, wagons, and other valuables, as well as money, clothing, etc., not one particle of which has been satisfactorily accounted for, and which, in my opinion, was distributed among the white inhabitants who participated in this affair.[47]

The massacre, in 1857, was one of the most explosive episodes in the history of the American West – not only were 120 men, women and children killed, but the United States and the Church of Jesus Christ of Latter-day Saints almost went to war. The church issued a statement on the role its members played in the killings in 2007 and opened its archives to three scholars – Richard E. Turley Jr., a Latter-day Saint historian, and Brigham Young University professors

---

47 Commissioner of Indian Affairs Report, 1859

Ronald W. Walker and Glen M. Leonard – for their book, Massacre at Mountain Meadows, published in 2008. But in the aftermath of the massacre, only one participant was brought to trial, and that was John D. Lee.

In April 1857, a Mormon apostle named Parley P. Pratt was murdered in Arkansas by the legal husband of one of Pratt's plural wives. Mormons in Utah took the news as another example of religious persecution and considered Pratt a martyr. They began stockpiling grain, anticipating a violent and apocalyptic encounter with the people they called "Americans." The Army, they believed, was about to invade the Utah Territory, (an invasion that did not come until the following year in the Utah War) and Young tried to enlist Paiute Indians from nearby Mountain Meadows in the fight. He also warned "mobocrats" to steer clear of Mormon territory or they'd be met by the Danites, who would form a line of defense in villages near Mountain Meadows. Then he declared martial law, making it illegal to travel through the territory without a permit.

The Baker-Fincher party was most likely unaware of the new requirement for a permit to cross Utah. They grazed their cattle on Mormons' land as they passed through, stoking anger. The Mormon attackers concluded that the emigrants had figured out their ruse – and feared that word of their participation would hasten an assault by the Army. It was then that militia commander William H. Dame ordered his men to leave no witnesses. The emigrants were to be "decoyed out and destroyed with the exception of the small children," who were "too young to tell tales," according to another militia commander, Major John H. Higbee who relayed the orders to Lee. On September 11, John D. Lee and a group of militiamen approached the camp under a white flag and offered a truce, with assurances that Lee and his men would escort the emigrants to safety in Cedar City. All they'd have to do is leave their livestock and possessions to the Paiutes. Having no good options, the emigrants, about 120 men, women, and children, laid down their weapons and followed Lee and the militia away from the camp in three groups – the last comprising adult males. It was over quickly. The Arkansas men were shot at point-blank range; the women and children ahead were slaughtered by bullets and arrows in an ambush party. No one over the age of seven survived. The victims were hastily buried. Locals auctioned off or distributed their possessions and took in the surviving 17 young children.[48]

The Army did arrive in Utah, in 1858, but no war ensued – Young and the Buchanan administration negotiated an agreement in which Young would give way to a new governor. The following year, troops led by Major James H. Carleton went to Mountain Meadows to investigate the killings and found the bones of "very small children." The soldiers gathered skulls and bones and erected a cairn (heap of stones) with the words, "Here 120 men, women, and children were massacred in cold blood early in September 1857. They were from Arkansas." They marked the site with a cross inscribed, "Vengeance is mine. I will repay, saith the Lord." Lee and the other leaders swore that they would never reveal their parts in the massacre, and Lee himself told Brigham Young that the Paiutes had been responsible for it – an explanation that became the official position of the LDS church for generations. In a report to Congress, Major Carleton blamed Mormon militiamen and church leaders for the massacre. Young excommunicated both Lee and Haight for their roles, but only Lee faced charges. After a first trial ended in a mistrial, Lee

---

48 Ronald W. Walker, Richard E. Turley, Glen M. Leonard, Massacre at Mountain Meadows, Oxford University Press, 2008.

was convicted in 1877 and sentenced to death by firing squad. Lee claimed that he was a scapegoat, and that other Mormons were more directly involved in the planning and in the killing. And although he maintained at first that Young was unaware of the massacre until after it took place, Lee would later state, in his *Life and Confessions of John D. Lee*, that the massacre occurred "by the direct command of Brigham Young." And on the morning of his execution, Lee would write that Young was "leading the people astray" and that he was being sacrificed "in a cowardly, dastardly manner." "I did everything in my power to save that people, but I am the one that must suffer," Lee wrote. He closed by asking the Lord to receive his spirit, and then he was taken to the massacre site. As many as 300 onlookers had gathered. On March 28, 1877, John Doyle Lee, wearing a coat and scarf, took a seat atop the coffin where his body would lie. A photographer was nearby. Lee asked that whatever photograph was made be copied for his last three wives. The photographer agreed. Lee posed. And then an hour before noon, he shook hands with the men around him, removed his coat and hat and faced the five men of the firing party. "Let them shoot the balls through my heart!" Lee shouted. "Don't let them mangle my body!" On U.S. Marshal William Nelson's command, shots rang out in the ravine where so many shots had rung out twenty years before, and Lee fell back onto his coffin, dead.

On April 20, 1961, a joint council was held with the First Presidency and the Council of Twelve Apostles of the Church of Jesus Christ of Latter-day Saints. "After considering all the facts available," the Church authorized "reinstatement to membership and former blessings to John D. Lee." The reinstatement puzzled many. But four decades later, the church claimed full responsibility for the incident that led to Lee's execution.[49]

At a memorial ceremony on September 11, 2007, the sesquicentennial anniversary of the Mountain Meadows Massacre, LDS Apostle Henry B. Eyring read the church's official statement to gatherers: *"We express profound regret for the massacre carried out in this valley 150 years ago today, and for the undue and untold suffering experienced by the victims then and by their relatives to the present time. A separate expression of regret is owed the Paiute people who have unjustly borne for too long the principal blame for what occurred during the massacre. Although the extent of their involvement is disputed, it is believed they would not have participated without the direction and stimulus provided by local church leaders and members."*

---

49 "Last Words and the Execution of John D. Lee, March 28, 1877," As reported by his attorney, William W. Bishop in Mormonism Unveiled; Or the Life and Confession of John D. Lee (1877.)

CHAPTER 13:

Reservations

In 1856 three farms were established, under the direction of Agent Hurt, on Corn Creek in Millard County, on Twelve-Mile Creek in San Pete County and on Spanish Fork Creek in Utah County. These "reservation" farms were established without the approval from the Federal Government. The farms were a failure and gradually deteriorated and disappeared. During their existence the Indians died from illness, starvation, and were murdered by the local white settlers. The Mormon plan for the native people was a lie, extermination was more expedient.

In 1857 Superintendent Young was released from his duties, an investigation began into his accounts as Indian Agent. The money, farm implements, and food supplies provided by the Federal Government were not received by the Indians. Superintendent Young doled out the majority to his followers to establish their settlements throughout the Utah Territory. More than three years later, the Federal Government closed Brigham Young's accounts and he was released from any wrongdoing. The Spanish Fork reservation, in Utah Valley, was commenced about four years ago, for a portion of the Utah Indians, which claim and have always lived in this valley. I have been endeavoring to induce the Uinta Tribe, or, at all events, a portion of them, to locate on this reservation. My efforts, so far, have proved unsuccessful. I held my last interview with them upon this subject the past month. They earnestly desired me to give them pork, cattle, and a few farming appliances to take to the Uinta, and to send a white man to instruct them in the art of husbandry. This farm and reservation are advantageously located in Utah Valley, bounded on the northwest, for four miles, by Utah lake, and several miles on the northeast by the Spanish Fork creek, both containing an abundance of trout and other fish.

The San Pete Valley farm is one hundred and fifty miles south of this city. This farm was intended for a band of Utahs, not exceeding eighty in number. Many more, however, visit the farm and receive assistance. The labor being principally performed by Indians; but the grasshoppers and crickets have nearly made a clean sweep of everything. The Corn Creek farm located in Fillmore Valley commenced about three years ago. The farms heretofore mentioned were not in a promising condition when I assumed their supervision. There were upon them scarce any farming appliances or work cattle, and the Indians for whom they were commenced were in a state of excitement and scattered and roaming through the southern settlements. Annoying them greatly. I have heretofore letters to the department, and in this report, adverted to the distressed condition of the Indians in this Territory generally, attributable to, there having been dispossessed by the whites of the land which produced for them the elements of life, and yet they have received no remuneration for any of their lands.

During the period of 1847 through about 1860, the Yutas of central Utah were pushed to the east of the Mormon communities and were forced to maintain themselves in decreasing territory, much of which was desert in the area between the Wasatch (Timpanogos) Mountains at Heber Valley and the Rocky Mountains to the East in Colorado. A large part of this high desert the Indians had previously only passed through while traveling between more productive hunting and gathering grounds. Reduction in the size and quality of areas available for support made it increasingly difficult for the Indians to maintain themselves in large groups. Bands began to fragment. Evidence of this social fragmentation is seen in the emergence of several previously, unheard of bands, such as Elk Mountain, Sheberetches and Seuvarits said to roam throughout eastern Utah.

Utah Superintendency
Office of the Superintendent of Indian Affairs, W.T.
(Great Salt Lake City, Utah Territory)

6 SEPTEMBER 1858

The tribes and fragments of tribes with whom I had business relations during my forced residence at Camp Scott are as follows, to wit: on the second day of December last I was visited by San-Pitch, a principal chief of the Utahs, and a few of his men. They wished to see Agent Hurt, who was then residing at Camp Scott. On the 10th of December following, Little Soldier, chief, and Benj. Simons, sub-chief, of a band of Sho-sho-nes, with some of their principal men, called on me. Their reason for visiting camp was to ascertain the object and ultimate destination of so many soldiers in the Territory. All this was explained to them, and after receiving some presents they departed for their homes in Weber Valley. About the 22d day of December last, I was visited at

Camp Scott, by White-eye and San-pitch, Utah chiefs, with several of their bands. They were destitute of provisions and almost in a starving condition, while it was not in my power to procure provisions for them, after making them some presents, I dismissed them, and they returned to their camp on Henry's fork. These Indians belong to one of the principal tribes of this Territory (Yutas or Utahs). There is but one other large tribe, (the Snakes,) as I am informed. Both the principal tribes are Shoshone and of course, are divided into a great number of small bands, but all submit to the authority of one of the chiefs of their respective tribes. Strenuous efforts will be made to induce this tribe (the Utahs) to locate permanently, as no permanent good can ever be done for them if they roam about in their wild state. I visited San-Pete creek farm last month, (August,) which is situated in the west end of San-Pete valley and county. This farm was opened about two years ago, under the direction of Agent Hurt, for a band of the Utahs under Chief Arapeen, a brother of San-Pitch. In my opinion, reservations should be made without delay. A farm was commenced several years ago for a small tribe called the Pah-vants, on Corn creek, in Millard County, under the direction of Agent Hurt. Ranosh (Kanosh), the chief of this tribe, visited me. His request was not as Indians generally are, for paint, beads etc., but for, agricultural implements.

For several years an enmity has existed between the Utahs and the Snakes. My attention was directed to this soon after entering upon my official duties. I alluded to the feud during my first interview with the Utahs, in December last, but their war-chief, White-eye, did not seem disposed to talk about it, and it was not until April last that they signaled their willingness to make peace with the Snakes. On the 3d day of May I received information that the Snake tribe of Indians were encamped on Green River. Reports were in circulation that they had come to make war upon the Utahs, who were encamped in the vicinity of Camp Scott. Immediately upon hearing the report, I dispatched a messenger to Wash-a-kee to learn his intentions, and if he intimated hostility to the Utahs to persuade him to encamp at some convenient place, until I could have a talk with him. On the 6th day of May my express man returned and informed me that Wash-a-kee was willing to leave the adjustment of the difficulties between his tribe and the Utahs to me. Accordingly, on the 13th of May, Wash-a-kee, of the Snakes, White-Eye, Son-a-at, and San-Pitch, of the Utahs, with sub-chiefs of the different tribes, and several chiefs of the Bannocks, assembled in council at Camp Scott, when, after considerable talk and smoking, peace was made between the two tribes. After I had given the Snakes and Bannocks some presents' they left camp.[50]

The Deseret News (Salt Lake City)
23 FEBRUARY 1859

A Memorial to Congress for an Act authorizing the purchase of Indian lands in Utah and locating the Indians on Reserves. To the Honorable, the Senate and House of Representatives of the United States, in Congress assembled: Your memorialists, the Governor and Legislative Assembly of the Territory of Utah, respectfully and earnestly petition your honorable body to pass an Act authorizing the Superintendent of Indian Affairs, or the appointment of a commission whose duty it shall be to treat with, and purchase, the lands belonging to the various tribes of Indians, situated in this Territory, to wit: The Shoshone or Snake, Pahvante, San Pitch, Piedes, Cummumbahs, or Snake Diggers, Uinta and Yampa Yutas (Utahs), and other bands; and that it shall be the duty of the said Superintendent or commission, to locate said

---

50 Commissioner Of Indian Affairs Report 1858 No. 78 Jacob Forney, Superintendent of Indian Affairs, W.T. to Hon. C.E. Mix, Commissioner of Indian Affairs, Washington, D.C.

Indians on reservations of land, at suitable distances from white set-tlers. Your memorialists do also respectfully petition your honorable body, to appropriate a sum sufficient to effect the treaties, purchases, removals, and locations contemplated in this memorial; and for estab-lishing schools, erecting mills, furnishing tools for labor and teachers for the Indians. Your memorialists respectfully represent, that the best tract of country, on which to locate the Indians within our Territory, is situated at the junction of the Bear and Little Snake rivers, where they may obtain plenty of fish, a comfortable supply of elk, antelope, deer, and buffalo, while the land is suitable for extensive cultivation, and possesses suitable mill sites. This location possesses the further advan-tages of being sufficiently near the white settlements for all purposes of trade and supervision; and it is sufficiently remote to prevent sud-den outbreaks from the Indians, or illegal trade by the settlers. In cases of hostility, the country is easily reconnoitered, and is within efficient striking distance of our garrisons; besides, while to the citizens it would afford all the benefits of an effectual removal, to the Indians it would possess scarcely the grievance of a removal at all, as in that region great numbers of the Indians have been accustomed to assembling. The early attention, and favorable consideration of your honorable body, to this very important subject is earnestly and respectfully solicited and your memorialists as in duty bound will ever pray.

Approved Jan. 12, 1859 – I certify that the foregoing is a true copy of the original on file in my office. John Hartnett, Secretary of Utah

Utah Superintendency (Great Salt Lake City)
29 SEPTEMBER 1859

The Indians, claiming a home in Utah Territory, are evidently the off-spring of two nations who migrated west of the Rocky Mountains from

the northwest many years ago. It is probable that most of the descendants of those nations are now within the boundary of this Territory.
They have greatly decreased in numbers, and proportionately in their
mental and physical condition, during the past thirty years. Their
degeneracy in the mode of living and comforts has been more manifest
during that period. This I learn, from the old mountaineers who have
lived among them, corroborated by Indian testimony. The descendants
of the two nations above alluded to are now called the Sho-sho-ne or
Snake, and the Utah or Yuta (there are no 'Utes' in Utah in 1859 - the
term "Ute" is a derogatory name the Mormons called all Indians. It
stems from the early Spanish explorers and means an unknown Indian
in Castilian Spanish). The only exception to these two primary nations
is a small tribe of Bannocks, numbering about five hundred. "Horn,"
the principal chief of these, with his people, visited Fort Bridger in April
1858, where I had an interview with them. I granted to this tribe of
Bannocks a home in the portion of this Territory claimed and inhabited by Wash-a-kee and his tribe of Sho-sho-nes, and with that chief's
entire consent. These two tribes are extensively intermarried and live
together amicably. The Utah, Pah-vant, and Pey-ute (Paiute), consti-
tute the second division of the Indians. Although these are designated
by several different names, yet they all emanate from one nation or
tribe, and speak the same language.

The Utahs are subdivided into several tribes and many bands.
Those known as Uinta-Utahs, claim Uinta Valley and the country
along the Green River. A portion of these have lived, part of last and
this summer at the Spanish Fork reservation. This tribe is governed by
four chiefs, and numbers about one thousand and, there is a band of
Utahs, with several chiefs, numbering about five hundred, who, is pursuant with my request, mostly located, late May, on the Spanish Fork

reservation, where it is presumed, they will continue. Another band of about eighty Utahs are living on the San-Pete Indian farm.

According to information received from the most reliable sources, Utah contains an Indian population of about 15,000, known as Utahs, San-Petes, Pah-Vants, and Pah-Utes. The three farms at Spanish Fork, San-Pete, and Corn Creek, which were commenced by my predecessor, were intended for the accommodation of those bands only whose lands had been at the time usurped and occupied by the white population. Settlements are still being extended over the Territory, and into valleys claimed and occupied by other bands, which must necessarily deprive them of their hunting grounds, and greatly impair their already too limited means of subsistence. The lands adapted for cultivation in the Territory are limited and are those best qualified for gratuitous support of its original inhabitants, being the only spots upon which they can subsist during the accumulate snows of winter, in the mountains. These localities, if permitted, will all soon be taken up by the white settlers; and what is to be the future destiny of these destitute creatures, is for the wisdom of Congress to determine.[51]

The Pah-vant are Yuta (Utah) Indians, but are a distinct, organized tribe and number about seven hundred. They obey and are controlled by one principal, and several sub-chiefs. About half of them have their home on the "Corn Creek" Indian farm. The other wing of the tribe lives along "Sevier Lake" and surrounding country, in the northeast extremity of Fillmore Valley, and about fifty miles from Fillmore City.

---

51 Commissioner of Indian Affairs Report No. 178, 1859, Utah Superintendency, Great Salt Lake City, September 30, 1859: A. Humphreys, Indian Agent to Jacob Forney, Esq., Superintendent of Indian Affairs, Great Salt Lake, U.T.

The supposed total number of Indians in Utah Territory is as follows:

Sho-sho-nes-4,500
Ban-nocks-500
Uinta Utahs-1,000
Spanish Fork and San Pete farms-900
Pah-vant-700
Pey-utes (Paiutes) (South)-2,200
Pey-utes (Paiutes) (West)-6,000
Elk Mountain Utes (Utahs)-2,000
Wa-sho of Honey lake-700

Total: 18,500

The Sho-sho-nes claim the northeastern portion of the Territory for about four hundred miles west, and from one hundred to one hundred and twenty-five miles south, from the Oregon line. The Utahs claim the balance of the Territory.

The Indians in Utah are extremely poor. The utmost ingenuity is put in requisition to sustain life; they eagerly seek after everything containing a life-sustaining element, such as hares, rabbits, antelope, deer, bear, elk, dogs, lizards, snakes, crickets, grasshoppers, ants, roots, grass-seeds, bark, etc. Many men, women, and children are entirely naked. With some of the Indians, stealing cattle, horses, mules, etc., is a matter of necessity – steal or starve.

It is my clear conviction that the immigration of a white population into the Territory has had disastrous effect upon the Indians. Game cannot exist except in the fertile watered valleys; these, with a few exceptions, are occupied by a thrifty population, and, consequently, the game is exterminated.

All the tribes and bands visited by me have received presents, such as baskets, various kinds of clothing, and ammunition: the last was not dealt out indiscriminately to some of the bands. I have given frequent material aid in flour, beef, etc., especially to those who have been forced to give up to the whites which furnished them with subsistence. About five bands of the Sho-sho-nes are severe sufferers by the influx of whites; those who inhabited Great Salt Lake, Weber, Bear, Cache, and Malad Valleys, extending eighty miles north. These valleys, which, in their natural state, furnished the Indians much subsistence, are now entirely occupied by permanent inhabitants. Game in this country must become extinct when valleys, adapted to farming purposes, are occupied by white men, which is already the case, with few exceptions: so much so, that it will be difficult, even now, to procure an advantageous location for a reservation for the Sho-sho-ne bands above alluded to, without paying for improvements.

With exception of the Uinta and Elk Mountain, the country of the Utahs is fast filling up with settlers. The government has, however, made three eligible Indian farms in the country claimed by the Utahs. The Uinta Utahs, the band at Spanish Fork, the one at San Pete, and the Pah-Vants, at Corn creek, have received much more assistance heretofore than all the other Indians in the Territory; and unless I am much deceived, these same Indians have been guilty of more depredations than any others in the Territory. It is gratifying, however, to be justified in saying that these Indians have done better this season than ever heretofore, and they promise fair for the future. I am endeavoring to have them permanently located on the several farms; and, until this is accomplished, no salutary improvement can be expected in their habits and condition.

CHAPTER 14:

1860's

The Mountaineer (Salt Lake City, Utah)
12 MAY 1860

Indian News – An-terro Vye-a-hoo, a Yampah Utah, and Tabby, son of old Euinta, have been in this city a few days. They say that in about two moons, there is going to be a great treaty between the Utahs and Snake nations. To complete the treaty the Utahs are to meet Wash-a-keek and his tribe at Yellow Creek, near the place where Walkara and the Snakes fought many years ago. Anterro says that five white men, who were engaged in prospecting for gold, have been killed the past winter by the Tao Utahs. A large encampment of the Yampah Utahs is just below the government camp at Camp Floyd and on the same creek. Saw-ey-ett and band are encamped at the mouth of Spanish Fork Canyon.

The Indians under my immediate control (or the most of them) are located upon three reservations among the white settlers, viz: Spanish Fork reservation, in Utah County; population 15,000. San

Pete reservation, in San Pete County; population 5,000; and Corn Creek reservation, in Millard County, (near Fillmore City, the former capital of the Territory), about 4,000. Thus, it will be seen that they are entirely surrounded by a large Mormon population extending over three counties, having no, sympathy or interest in them, which deprives them of all chances of killing games, even for their partial subsistence and leaves them destitute of any other source from whence to kook for the commonest necessaries of life than the government; and here I would state that in consequence of the great damage to their crops by grasshoppers and crickets in 1859, the suffering of these poor Indians during the past winter were horrible, many of them dying from starvation and exposure. It was a common circumstance to find them frozen to death. I made frequent requisitions upon and earnest appeals to the Superintendent. He steadily refused to relieve their sufferings, notwithstanding he had in his possession at the time some $5,000 or $6,000 worth of Indian goods. I was compelled to witness the suffering and death of these poor creatures, without money, provisions, or clothing where with to relieve them. On several occasions I parted with my own blankets to bury them in.[52]

On the 3d of May Superintendent Forney received information that the Snake tribe was encamped on the Green River, and they had come to make war upon the Utahs, who were encamped in the vicinity of Camp Scott. He dispatched a message to Wash-a-kee to learn of his intentions. Accordingly, on the 13th of May Wash-a-kee, of the Snakes; White-eye, Son-a-at and San-Pitch, of the Utahs; with the sub-chiefs of the different tribes, and several chiefs of the Bannocks assembled in council at Camp Scott. After considerable

---

52 Commissioner of Indian Affairs Report, No. 76, Novenber12, 1860: A. H Humphreys, Indian Agent, Utah Territory to Hon. Charles E. Mix, Acting Commissioner of Indian Affairs, Washington D.C.

talk and smoking, peace was made between the two tribes. The Indians, claiming a home in Utah Territory, are evidently from the offspring of two nations who migrated west of the Rocky Mountains from the Northwest many years ago. It is probable that most of the descendants of those nations are now within the boundary of this Territory. They have greatly decreased in numbers, and proportionately in their mental and physical condition, during the past thirty years. Their degeneracy in the mode of living and comforts has been more manifest during that period. This I learn from old mountaineers who have lived among them, corroborated by Indian testimony. The descendants of the two nations above alluded to are now called Sho-sho-ne or Snake, and Utah or Ute (this term was not appropriate for the Utahs).[53]

An 1860 report by government Indian Agents noted that many of the Indians that stayed near government created farms (located in the Salt Lake Valley) in the winter of 1859-1860 died of starvation and cold. There were many other reports noting a marked decline in the population of the 'Yutas' in Utah during this period.

Death of Arapeen (Manti, Sanpete County)
9 DECEMBER 1860

ED. Deseret News: The Utah Chief Arapeen died on Tuesday last, the 4th instant, about sixty miles south of this place. He was on his return from the Navajo country where he had been on a trafficking expedition, together with many of his tribe or band. He died with good feelings towards the whites in this Territory for their hospitality to him and his people and requested that no person should be killed on account of his death. I had a visit this morning from his brother Sanpitch and ten

---

53 Commissioner of Indian Affairs Report No. 174 from J. Forney, Superintendent Indian Affairs.

others of the tribe. He is at present the leader of the band, and wishes, as well as his men, to be at peace with all. They mourn the loss of Arapeen. Sanpitch states that he had four of his brother's horses and five of his cattle killed after he died. He wants the Superintendent to come up this way with some of his presents, if he has not given them all to "Little Soldier," the pe-up captain. He wishes to have Arapeen's death published in the papers.

In 1861, the territories of Nevada and Colorado were created in whole or in part from Utah Territory, and an addition to the territory of Nebraska was made. Further portions of the territory were allocated to Nevada in 1862 and 1866 and to Wyoming in 1868. These events formed the present borders of the state of Utah. A third effort by the Mormons to acquire statehood occurred in 1862, but serious consideration was not given by Congress because legislation prohibiting plural marriage was in the process of being enacted. The fourth attempt, occurring in 1876 was unsuccessful, because executive and legislative leaders pronounced that statehood was not possible, as long as, plural marriage continued to be condoned and practiced in the territory of Utah. In 1882, the territorial legislature devised a new plan to obtain statehood. The plan entailed the request of a republican form of government that provided the citizens of the Utah Territory with the liberties sought by the founding fathers of the nation. Although the Mormons presented appropriate legislation to Congress, the request was ignored. In 1887, a sixth organized effort for statehood was initiated that involved the submission of a state constitutional clause that recognized polygamy as incompatible with a republican form of government. This elaborate attempt at statehood met the same fate as its predecessors. After six unsuccessful bids for statehood were made between 1849 and 1887, Mormon leaders realized that the unsettled separation of church-state conflict needed to be resolved in order to be admitted to the union.

The Deseret News (SLC)
3 APRIL 1861

Visit from the Utahs: The Utah Chief, Peteetneet, who has become the leader or principal chief of his band, since the death of Arapeen, accompanied by Sanpitch and some twenty other Indians of their tribe, came into the city on Friday last, to see the Superintendent; get some presents etc., and remained hereabouts two or three days. Colonel Davies is reported to have received them very kindly, and gave them blankets and many other presents, with which they were highly pleased. The chiefs dined with him once or twice and went away very favorably impressed with his demeanor and generous treatment to them and their braves. After donning their new blankets, they walked about the streets quite majestically, and when they took their departure for their mountain haunts, they felt much better than they would if they had been treated as savages as they too often are, by government representatives.

The Deseret News (Salt Lake City, Utah)
1 MAY 1861

The Uinta Indians – Tsha-we-unt White Eye, the principle or head chief of the Utahs, accompanied by about twenty lodges of the Uinta band, arrived at the Spanish Fork Indian farm, on Friday last, intending, as reported by Mr. D.B. Huntington, Indian Interpreter, to remain there during the summer. They should be sent back to their own country, by the Superintendent without delay, as they will have to be sustained by the whites while they remain there, but when on their hunting grounds they can support themselves. The old chief came to the city on Sunday to see the Superintendent, and get some presents, and remained a day or two and then returned to the farm, well satisfied with his visit. The sojourning of Indians from other and distant valleys should not be tolerated in the settlements, and if the government agents do their duty, White Eye and his attendants will be sent back to Colorado instanter.

The Deseret News (Salt Lake City, Utah)
1 MAY 1861

As stated in a previous report, I arrived here on the 11th day of November 1860. The time for active farming operations had expired, and winter in this region had set in. The farms at the San Pete, Corn Creek, Deep Creek, and Ruby Valley reserves had been abandoned by my predecessor and gone to ruin; and the various tribes attached thereto had wandered off and returned to their mountain haunts. The Indians were in a state of nakedness and starvation, destitute of shelter, and dying of want. Owing to a previous state of facts, known to the department, the Indians lost confidence in the government and people of the United States, had become vicious and spiteful. I made arrangement's; to reach and bring in all the petty of the chiefs of that once powerful tribe, with their followers, who kept secreted in the mountains and deserts; and Green Jacket, Teekutup, Jack, Tabby, and their bands, have traveled hundreds of miles to see me, and have spent several days each at my quarters. For the various bands of Utahs, Pah-Utes, Pah-Vants, and others who congregate at the Spanish Fork farm, I recommend the establishment of a reserve, including the whole of Winter Valley (Uinta Valley) in addition to the Spanish Fork, Corn Creek, and San Pete reserves.

The destitution of these Indians and the excessive severity of the wintry seasons caused much sickness, especially inflammatory and pulmonary diseases among them. Great suffering and many deaths transpire, which might be mitigated, and perhaps prevented, by proper medical treatment. The Indians of Utah, although the poorest and most helpless on the continent, are not so demoralized and corrupted as those who have been brought into closer association with the white men in other localities. Infidelity of the wife, or prostitution of an unmarried female is punishable by death, and but few such acts transpire among them.[54]

In recent consultations or "talks" with Wash-a-kee and Sho-kub, the head chiefs of the Shoshones or Snake Indians, Navacoots and Pe-tut-neet chiefs of the Utah Nation, and many sub-chiefs of both nations, I find that they are unanimously in favor of a treaty with the United States and agree with me in considering that to be the only effectual way to check the stealing propensities of some of their Indians. They express their willingness to cede to the United States all the lands they claim in the Territory, except for reservations necessary for their homes. They seem to fully understand the nature and effect of a treaty. They seem fully to understand the nature and effect of a treaty, and the chiefs agree to hold themselves responsible for any depredations committed by any of their bands, if a treaty should be made, by deducting the amount of damage done from the annuity paid them. As soon as practicable after my arrival here, I made a visit to the Spanish Fork Indian farm and reservation, in order to ascertain from personal observation, the extent of the improvements there, and estimate the amount necessary to carry on farming for the benefit of the Indians at that place. There was no one living on the farm at the time of my visit. I found everything in a very dilapidated condition,

---

54 Commissioner of Indian Affairs Report No. 49, 1861, Utah Superintendency, Utah Territory, June 30, 1861: Benjamin Davies, Superintendent of Indian Affairs, Utah Territory to Hon. Wm P. Dole, Commissioner of Indian Affairs, Washington, D.C.

the place having been cleared of everything that was salable, to buy food for the Indians that congregate around here.[55]

Sir, in compliance with your request, I proceeded immediately to the Corn Creek Indian reservation in Millard County, in this Territory, and examined the Indian farm on said reservation. There are no improvements upon the farm whatever, further than ploughing, except a small double log cabin, very much out of repair. These Indians, the Pah-Utes, are very industrious, and solicit the aid of the government, in the strongest terms, in their behalf. They complain most bitterly of your predecessors holding out inducements and making them many promises which they never fulfilled. If any Indians are entitled to and merit the aid of the government, they are these. I was further informed that Major Humphreys had taken many of the implements, such as ploughs, hoes, harrows, and wagons, from this as well as the San Pete Indian reservation, and disposed of them. This has quite discouraged the poor Indians, which causes them to ask if the great father has thrown them away.[56]

Sir: For answer to your letter dated May 3, 1861, requesting my opinion concerning the disposal of certain worthless animals, at the various reserves of Corn Creek, San Pete, and Spanish Fork, and the destitution of the Indians thereat, I have to say that I am entirely destitute of funds, and am unable to supply any means to subsist them. Of their destitutions I am well advised; and if they are not furnished means to live, they must and will commit depredations to subsist themselves. If the necessary supplies are not furnished to me very shortly, I shall deem it my duty to repair to the seat of our national government, and lay the state of

---

55 Commissioner of Indian Affairs Report No. 50, 1861, Office of the Superintendent of Indian Affairs, Great Salt Lake City, Utah Territory, October 1, 1861.

56 Commissioner of Indian Affairs Report 1861, Dyman S. Wood, Indian Agent to Major H. Martin Superintendent of Indian Affairs, Utah Territory, October 1, 1861.

the case, as existing here before the proper department. In the meantime, I have to advise that you sell and dispose of all useless articles first, and resort to every means at your command to feed and preserve quiet and order among them, until headquarters can be heard from.[57]

Sir: Some of the citizens of this Territory have, within the past fifteen days, caused to be surveyed and located with the avowed intention of settling and cultivating, a part of this Spanish Fork reservation, my notice to desist to the contrary notwithstanding. You will please instruct me as to the proper course to pursue in the premises.

The Indians are exceedingly poor, not less than five hundred of them depending entirely upon the government for food and clothing on account of the almost entire absence of game for them to subsist upon, and absolutely must be cared for and provided with subsistence by the government; and if this be withheld absolute want will impel them to the commission of depredations, and an Indians war will inevitably follow.

Whites (Mormons) have been permitted to take possession of all the valleys in the Territory, wherein, heretofore, the Indians were enabled to procure a subsistence. It is true, however, that the government has set apart three small reservations, to wit: Spanish Fork, containing about fifteen thousand acres, but surrounded by a large Mormon population, who have no particular regard for the welfare of the Indians, from the fact that they have surveyed said reservation with the avowed intention of taking possession of it, as my letter to the department dated July 2, 1861, will show, Corn Creek reservation is yet small, closely surrounded by white settlements, which renders it very nearly valueless as an Indian reservation, because of the Indians continually coming into contact with the whites. San Pete reservation is

---

57 Commissioner of Indian Affairs Report 1861, Benjamin Davies, Superintendent of Indian Affairs, Great Salt Lake City, U.T. May 6, 1861. to A. Humphries, Indian Agent.

worthless and abandoned by the superintendent in the spring of 1860. Winter Valley (Uinta Valley) has been recently set apart for the benefit of the Indians; and a more humane scheme thus proposed could not have been devised by the government. It is, in fact, the only place of resort for a very large number of Indians. This valley is extensive in size, and fertile. It will make, with the proper improvements, a fine farming country, besides which, part of the Indians will be removed a hundred miles from the white settlements – proving, thereby, beneficial to both races. It may be proper here to state that there is a question as to whether the government agents will be permitted to hold and occupy this valley as a reservation, notwithstanding the government has set it apart for the benefit of the Indians, for the reason that the Mormon people, on the 5th instant, were sending out a large emigration of settlers for the purpose of taking possession of it, said to be done by the order of President Young, their prophet. If the settlers should persist in its occupation and retention, it will be impossible for the government officials to do anything without sufficient force wherewith to sustain themselves. Brigham Young is absolute, so also is his decree, the government's wishes to the contrary notwithstanding, unless more loyal counsels should prevail.[58]

In January of 1861, Utah Territory was partitioned by the United States Government to create Colorado Territory that took in the east and west face of the Rocky Mountains. The four bands of Paiute Indians who are part of the Confederated Ute Bands of Colorado would not arrive in Colorado Territory until 1863 from New Mexico Territory.

Subsequently these four bands of Southern Paiutes were enjoined with the three small bands of White Rivers that are mixed

---

58 Commissioner of Indian Affairs Report, No.53, 1861, A. Humphries, Indian Agent, Utah to Hon. William P. Dole, Commissioner of Indian Affairs Washington D.C., September 30, 1861.

Comanche Arapaho Plains Indians who had an unratified treaty of 1866 when they were enjoined in the Treaty of 1868 with the Southern Paiutes, whereby, the seven bands were collectively called by the United States the "Confederated Bands of Ute Indians of Colorado".

The Colorado Indians known as "Utes" are a separate tribe with no ancient or historic affiliations with the Utah and Snake bands of Shoshone Indians.

The Uinta River Valley Basin Reservation was set apart for the Utah Indians, separated from the public domain by an Executive Order issued by President Abraham Lincoln in 1861. It was confirmed by the Senate on May 5, 1864 (13 Stat. 63) and was settled by various bands and family clans of Utah and other Shoshone Indians, some fleeing from the white settlers in the Salt Lake Valley of the Great Basin in Western Utah. Eventually these Shoshone bands of Utahs amalgamated in the Uinta Valley Basin as a single Tribe of Uinta Valley Shoshone Indians or "Uinta Band". When it was acquired by the United States in 1848, their ancestors had historically occupied the entire Utah Territory. The early bands called themselves Utahs, as documented by the various Spanish explorers, Indian agents, and Federal Government documents. The territory was named after them and eventually when Utah was approved for statehood, the name was kept. Keeping the Utah Shoshone legacy alive throughout history.

Daily Missouri Republican (St. Louis, Missouri)
18 MAY 1861

Indians and Other Folks – Uinta's son and Black Hawk came in on Thursday from the Pi-ed country to see the representative of the Great Father at Washington. They came about four hundred miles from the south, and got a few notions, and left again yesterday morning. They passed Nampudes, a Utah, on his return from the Elk Mountains to Spanish Fork. Nampudes reports that the Paw-Utes and Navajos had joined and had a brush with the United States soldiers, who had been sent out to chastise the Navajos for their attack on the Butterfield mail some time back, Uncle Sam's boys are said to have got wiped out. Young Uinta and Black Hawk report their own people dreadfully afflicted. Consumption and bloody flux were carrying them off rapidly. Tsi-Gwitch, from the north, and Ammon and band, from the South, have also visited our great city during the week. Something, if not worse than consumption and bloody flux, quite as perplexing, is very prevalent among the Indians generally, who have had the misfortune, to come in contact with civilization. At Shell Creek, Spring Valley, and Deep Creek and stations adjoining, the Indians are literally starving. They are complaining sadly about want of attention. About two hundred braves assembled two weeks at one of the stations, expecting to meet the Superintendent, who had promised to see them again "when the grass grew." The grass is growing out West; but the speech is not yet perfected, and the Indians must rove hungry and faint, and forced to subsist by theft, and then be punished for transgression.

The Deseret News (Salt Lake City, Utah)
19 JUNE 1861

Uinta Indians – White Eye and Antero, with some others of their tribe who have been at the Spanish Fork Farm most of the time this spring, came in and took a look at the News printing establishment on Monday last. They intend returning to their own country on the Colorado shortly. A letter dated June 30, 1861, from Superintendent Benjamin Davies to Commissioner Dole describes the conditions of the Yutas' when Davies arrived in Utah in early 1861 as in a "state of naked-ness, and starvation, destitute and dying of want." Many 'Yutas' died of exposure and starvation during the winters of 1859-60 and 1860-61. Hubert Bancroft describes these times by stating: "The natives had no alternative but to steal or starve; the white man was in possession of their pastures; game was rapidly disappearing, in the depth of winter they were starving and almost unclad, sleeping in the snow and sleet, with no covering but a cape of rabbit fur and moccasins (sic) lined with cedar bark." The following events leading up to the creation of the Uinta River Valley Reservation is taken from the history of Brigham Young whereby he writes: "The telegraphic dispatch from the East which came in by mail today brought the following paragraph dated, Washington, October 9th. "Brigham Young has lost Uinta Valley, one of the most fertile in Utah, after having announced his intention to settle it with the Saints. The President, by an order dated October, has directed an Indian reservation to be made there."

On Sunday August 25, a company of about 200 efficient men were called to go and make a settlement in the Uinta Valley, which had always been represented the finest valley in the Territory. Surveyor General Fox and, several pioneers were sent ahead to explore the country, soon an express arrived from the explorers, stating that the Valley had been misrepresented, and was not adapted to sustain large settlements, which statement was confirmed by the party on their return. On receiving the express, President Young had it read to the meeting in the Bowery, when he publicly announced the abandon-ment of the project. Mr. Martin, Superintendent of Indian Affairs for the Territory, on hearing of the proposed enterprise immediately wrote to the commissioner of Indian Affairs informing him of the same and recommending the setting a part of the valley and vicinity for an Indian reservation, to prevent the Mormons from settling there.[59]

On October 3, 1861, President Abraham Lincoln created the Indian reservation in the Uinta River Valley Basin. The area of the reservation recommended in the October 03, 1861, letter from Secretary of the Interior Smith approved by President Lincoln in creating the reserve (yet, unoccupied by settlement of our citizens) included "the entire Valley of the Uinta River within Utah Territory, extending on both sides of said river to the crest of the first range of mountains on each side…" An area of approximately 5.5 million acres of mostly high desert land "for the permanent settlement and exclusive occupancy" of the tribes of Utah Territory, located in the northeastern corner of what is now the State of Utah. The Uinta Valley Basin Reservation was confirmed by Congress. The 'Yuta' Shoshone Indians who settled on the reservation after 1861 lost their previous 'band' identity as they were forced into the reservation and subsequently amalgamated as the "Uinta Band" (a.k.a., Uinta Valley Shoshone Tribe of 'Yuta' Indians) a geographic location name given to them by Indian agents of the time. Nothing was done to encourage the Indians in the Salt Lake Valley to move to the Uinta Basin Reservation some 200 miles east until the Executive Order 38-1 was ratified by the Senate on May 5, 1864. Even after the confirmation, Congress initially provided inadequate funding to support the Uintas. The May 5, 1864, statute ratified the executive order 38-1 and directs the sale of all Indian reserves (farms) in the territory of Utah, except the Uinta River Valley Basin Reservation. The sale of the farms was later repealed by the Act of June 18, 1878, which directed the Secretary of the Interior to "restore the same to the public domain for disposition as other public lands.

---

59 History of Brigham Young, J. Willard Marriot Library, University of Utah.

Brigham Young and the Mormon settlers in Utah Territory in 1861 did not make a claim to any part of the Uinta River Valley Basin Indian Reservation or object to the Land Grant given by President Lincoln in allodial ownership exclusively to said Shoshone Indians in 1861. A disgruntled Brigham Young saying the Uinta River Basin was only fit for nomadic Indians and to hold the rest of the world together. The Reservation was confirmed by the United States of America, un-opposed, on May 5, 1864. Utah and its citizens, thereafter, are barred forever, by law, from making any governmental or private claim to said historic Uinta River Valley Basin Reservation Land, and all appurtenant thereto.

**The Confederated Bands of Ute Indians are officially located in Colorado Territory at this point in Territorial partitioning.

The Deseret News (Salt Lake City, Utah)
23 OCTOBER 1861

Office, Indian Affairs, G.S.L. City, U.T., Oct. 14th, 1861
To the Editor of The Deseret News, Great Salt Lake City

Sir: – I, (Henry Martin, Superintendent) deem it due to myself and the citizens of this Territory to make a frank and free explanation of my position in relation to certain charges, published in the New York Herald of 20th September last, claimed to be taken from my correspondence with the Indian Department at Washington. To fully explain my communication, I will first state the article entire that I refer to, which is as follows: "The Commissioner of Indian Affairs received to-day important advice from Indian Agent, Martin, dated Salt Lake City, September 3rd. He states that he can, with the present appropriations, easily take care of the Indians in his superintendency, so far as keeping them from committing any further depredations on emigrants, the

Overland Mail Company, or the Telegraph Line. They have been very hostile and unruly, from the fact that there is not hunting and fishing in Utah Territory to support them without help from the Indian Department, which he says he is satisfied they have not received. He, says further, that he can take care of, and protect the Telegraph and Overland Mail Company in the Territory of Utah, without the help of troops, but that they are to take care of the Mormons. He says, Brigham Young gave notice some days ago in church, that he intended to send about one hundred and fifty families to settle in Uinta Valley. He says it is of the utmost importance that the Government declare that section as Indian reservation, to prevent Mormons settling there. He says the Mormons are declaring their design to separate from the United States and erect their Territory into an independent province. The Mormon's further declare that no more Government trains shall pass through their Territory hereafter. The Government has taken measures to meet this difficulty."

Consistent with my instructions, as Superintendent of Indian Affairs for this Territory, and with my sense of duty, immediately on my arrival, I sought for information as to the true state and condition of the Indians in this Territory. My inquiries of the persons with whom I had official duties and others with whom I came in contact, led me to the conclusion that for the protection of the Mail and Telegraph troops were perfectly uncalled for, and could only be a benefit to contractors at a great risk of general evil to the Indians and citizens of the Territory. At the same time certain parties from the East, sympathizing with, if not avowed secessionists took the trouble to represent that a party was forming in Colorado Territory, for the purpose of cutting off all communication between the East and West, insinuating that if the secessionists succeeded in their scheme the people here would be induced to declare their independence. The excitement created by such statements *together with the malicious representations of a late Indian official, led me to make statement in private communications to a friend of mine in the Indian Department, that I have since found to be very errone-ous. The representations that had been made to the Indian Department by one of its late agents here, had left to my receiving instructions to prevent any imposition upon the rights of the Indians – hence when I learned of the Mission to Uinta, I conceived it my duty to request of the Department its instructions in the premises. I find, by further inves-tigation of that matter, that it is unnecessary and impolitic to, in any way, interfere with that valley. I also deny having made, in any form, the statements that the Mormons said no more Government trains should pass through the Territory, and further, that they were about to declare their independence.*

While I state the circumstances and associations which led to my writing as much as I have written, I disclaim any malicious inten-tion to injure the people here. I beg further to say, that I regret hav-ing written before I had personal knowledge of the people and of their intentions, but when the many mis-statements heretofore made to the people of the United States in regard to the citizens of this Territory are considered, it is not a subject of surprise that I and others should have been so easily inclined to lend an ear to listen to the present false charges against such citizens, and foolishly give credence to this mali-cious- statements. I most sincerely regret precipitancy in writing, and as far as I may be favored with an opportunity, hope to properly rep-resent the citizens of Utah as a law-abiding and peaceful community, as my subsequent intercourse with the people satisfies me that my for-mer statements and surmising, they were entirely unfounded. If, sir, you will give this communication publication, you will greatly oblige. Yours, Henry Martin, Superintendent

An exploration of Uinta Valley confirms the information heretofore given the department of its adaption to the purposes for which it has been reserved. Antero, a principal Utah Chief from Uinta Valley, and his band of twenty lodges, were last month on a visit of ceremony to the superintendent. In an interview, and in reply to my inquiries, he said the valleys of the Uinta and its branches are as good, or better, for cultivation as the valley of Salt Lake; that there is plenty of pine and cottonwood in the vicinity of the streams, and the best grass on the hills and in the bottoms; that his home is on the north fork of Uinta, where he has lived many years, and there is very little snow there. He has four cows, one of his bands; has eight, and they have several horses; and he asked that they may be given more stock – cows, oxen, mares, sheep, and hogs – and that a house may be built for him there, where he wishes to permanently reside. He has no doubt many of his band would soon follow his example, if they did not at once join him. He said he was ashamed to talk with me about settling there with his band, and having a house and more stock, as Dr. Hurtt and all the agents have heretofore promised him this for years past, but still, he has none; that he is no beggar.

I beg leave to adopt the views of the Commissioner contained in his annual report of last year, regarding, "cattle husbandry", by all the Indians in this Territory and hope the system may be commenced this fall in Uinta Valley with the Utahs and with the Shoshones, at such points as may be hereafter selected. These people are naturally inclined to a pastoral life, and if they can now receive the aid and encouragement of government, it is believed the most of the Utahs may be collected and permanently settled either in Uinta Valley or vicinity of the Colorado, south of this Territory, near the Mojaves, as was suggested in a former communication, where a large reservation can be made without interference with the white settlements already formed. Whenever they are established, a military post upon the reservation is deemed necessary (garrisoned by two or more companies) to maintain order, and to protect the Indians and the officers of government, and the reservation itself, from intrusions by white settlers. I feel it to be my duty to again recommend that treaties be entered into with all these tribes to extinguish their right of occupancy. Justice and the peace of the country require it and it seems to be necessary to bring them under the control of government, and to give proper effect to the laws of the Territory, and to those regulating Indian trade and Intercourse. Although the title was obtained by the treaty with Mexico, these Indians were then occupants of every portion of this Territory, enjoying the same rights and privileges as the Indians east of the Mississippi River. The United States accepted of the cession, subject to all the just rights of this third party then in the actual possession, but who was not party to the treaty.[60]

Sir: On the 20th of August I left this city to execute your orders, previously received, to make an examination of the valleys of the Uinta River and its tributaries, with a view to their adaptability for a settlement therein of the Utah Indians. This is a fine location, and is the one designated by Antero, one of the Utah Chiefs, as the place where he wished a house built for himself, this is a beautiful valley of very superior grass and grazing land, we were again on the summit of the Wausatch Mountains – the "divide" between the waters of Great Salt Lake and the Gulf of California. This is also the western boundary of the Uinta Reservation. The Uinta Indian reservation is entirely free from white settlers. It may be considered – the bottoms, the table land, and even the mountains – as a fine grazing country. The valleys are as I have described. It is well watered and abundantly

---

60 Commissioner of Indian Affairs Report, No. 39 September 12,1862. James Duane Doty, Superintendent to Hon. W.P. Dole, Commissioner of Indian Affairs.

timbered…I consider it most admirably adapted for the permanent location of the Indians in small settlements on its various streams. Of course, an agent would be required to reside in their midst, whose proper location would unquestionably be on the Uinta River, at the place designated by Chief Antero for his residence.[61]

In the month of July 1861, the Central Overland Mail Company fitted out an expedition under the command of Mr. Berthoud, known as one of the best engineers in the Pike's Peak gold region, with the old mountaineer, Major Bridger, as guide, for the purpose of exploring a new route for a road from Denver City to Salt Lake City. This route lay westward by the sources of the Blue and Yampah Rivers, and through the Colorado and Uinta Valley we saw no Indians upon the entire route until we reached Provo, on Utah Lake, although the whole distance passed was in the country of the Utahs.[62]

Within my agency proper, if I understand it correctly, there are five different tribes of Indians: Utahs, Shoshones, Goshee Utes, Par Vans, and Pie Edes, and each is divided onto several bands, with chiefs, besides several small bands with sub-chiefs. The Utahs are divided into six bands, of which Sowyett, White Eye, Tabby, Antero, Jo, and Kibe are their chiefs. Kibe's (or mountain) band is the only one that makes their permanent residence at this reservation, who are the remains of the two once powerful bands of Wakara and Pee-te-neete…they number 275 souls. It is also the concentrating point for all the different bands of Utahs once or twice per year. Immediate steps should be taken to remove trespassers upon this reservation who have built houses and taken up a permanent residence, or

---

61 Commissioner of Indian Affairs Report, September 12,1862. Amos Reed, Clerk of Superintendency to Hon. James Duane Doty, Superintendent of Indian Affairs, Utah Territory.

62 (Extract from E.D. Berthoud's journal of his trip from Denver City to Utah Lake,1861, by J.D. Doty)

surveyed out farms thereon, which is a great outrage upon the Indian department and agent. Sowyett's band, whose hunting grounds are at Uinta Valley, number 210 souls. Too much praise cannot be said of them. Their influence to suppress the evil, conduct of the vicious is immense, and never wanting. Antero and Tabby bands inhabit, most of the year, at Uinta Valley also, and sustain themselves mostly by hunting and fishing. They number about 300 souls, who seem to be peaceable and well disposed, and some of them could be induced to settle and labor. White eye band, whose hunting grounds are upon the Green River, makes a visit to this place once or twice a year for presents. They number 102 souls. They seem to be orderly and well disposed, and no Indian is allowed to live in their camp who will not obey the instructions of their chief, which are good and against immorality. Jo's band is in and about San Pete reservation, who claim great negligence on the part of the government.

Par Vans and Pie Edes I have not visited, having no means of conveyance, but seem to have been credibly informed of the extreme poverty of the Pie Edes, and their great desire to be assisted in cultivation of lands, and to become agriculturists.[63]

The Deseret News (SLC)
14 JUNE 1864

The Indian Treaty: As will be seen by perusing the correspondence on President Young's trip to Utah county, quite a large body of Indians were assembled at the Indian Farm near Spanish Fork, last week, to meet with the Presidential and Colonel Irish, Superintendent of Indian Affairs, to consider the terms of a treaty involving their title to the

---

63 Commissioner of Indian Affairs Report, No. 41, September 16, 1862, T.W. Hatch, Indian Agent to Hon. James D. Doty, Superintendent of Indian Affairs, Utah Territory.

Reservations in this Territory. Meetings were held with the Indians on Wednesday, Thursday and Friday, 7th, 8*th*, and 9th inst. On the first-named day a prepared abstract of the treaty was read by Colonel Irish, which is very liberal in its conditions and provisions. The Indians are required to move to Uinta Valley within one year from the ratification of the treaty, giving up their title to the Indian lands in Utah Territory; they are required to be peaceful, not to go to war with other bands or tribes except in self-defense, not to steal or molest the whites, to assist in cultivating the lands and to send their children to schools to be established for them. On abiding these conditions, the protection of the U.S. Government will be extended to them. Government will pay them $25,000 annually for the first ten years, $20,000 annually for the next twenty years and $15,000 annually for the thirty years thereafter. Farms will be made, a grist and lumber mill built, schools established, houses built for the principal chiefs, annuities paid to the chiefs, and other provisions of a beneficial character are guaranteed. The Indians are likewise to have the right of hunting, digging roots and gathering berries on all unoccupied lands, to fish in their accustomed places and erect houses for the purpose of curing fish. Several bands of the Utahs, the Pah-vants and the Timpanogs were present and represented by their chiefs, as was also the Cum-mum-bahs. Fifteen chiefs signed the treaty on Thursday, after a very interesting "talk" with them that morning and on the previous day. On Thursday afternoon, Colonel Irish distributed a large quantity of presents to them, having then seated in three rows opposite the farmhouse, the braves in one row, the squaws and papooses in another and the children in a third. Blankets, leggings, knives, tobacco, dresses, shirts, pants for the chiefs, etc., etc., were received with child-like eagerness by many, and with a sort of stoical apathy by some of the chiefs, who seemed to feel they should rest on their dignity to a certain extent. Good feelings prevailed among them, *and many expressions relative to their amicable relations in the past with the settlers were indulged in. The only chief who was averse to signing the treaty was San-pitch, brother to Wakara and Arrapeen, but subsequently it appeared more as if he were standing on his dignity as a "big chief" than anything else, he was willing to sign on Saturday, but the paper had then gone. He will have an opportunity of attaching his mark to the document. The chiefs manifested a strong sense of the justice of punishing the guilty for the crimes and misdemeanors, and not punishing the innocent for the evil deeds of the guilty, whether white or red. As a faithful observance of their treaties has ever been a characteristic of the Indians here as well as elsewhere, we have no doubt of their honorably keeping this, if it is not infringed upon by reckless whites.*

Black-hawk and his band, who have been perpetrating the late atrocities in that neighborhood, are still in the mountains, but effective measures are being adopted, we understand, to prevent a recurrence of them. Those who signed the treaty appeared favorably disposed to render assistance in that direction. The provisions of the treaty, and the opportunity of signing it, will be extended to the Indians throughout the entire Territory as early as possible.

CHAPTER 15:

Spanish Fork Treaty

In 1865, the white settlers continued to trespass on reservation lands in Ashley Valley, violating the 1861 Executive Order boundaries and squatting on Yuta-Shoshone lands. The problem was so prolific that the Indian Affairs Superintendent, O. H. Irish had the following Presidential injunctive order printed throughout the territorial newspapers, telling the white settlers to leave the Uinta Reservation.

The Union Vedette (Salt Lake City)
1865

NOTICE IS HEREBY GIVEN, that under an order of the President of the United States, dated October 3, 1861, the "entire portion of the valley of the Uinta River within Utah Territory, extending on both sides of said river to the crest of the first range of contiguous mountains on each side," was directed to be set apart as an Indian Reservation. That, by the provisions of an Act of Congress, approved May 5, 1864, the

Uinta Valley Reservation is 'set apart for the permanent settlement and exclusive occupation of such of the different tribes of Indians of Utah Territory as may be induced to inhabit the same'. Therefore, notice is hereby given under instructions of the Department of the Interior, transmitted to me through the Commissioner of Indian Affairs, "that all white settlers must forthwith remove from the Uinta Reservation," and that on the opening of spring all persons found therein unlawfully, that is, without a license to trade, a passport, or permission of the proper authority, will be removed, and that the laws of the United States, applicable to Indian Reservations, will be enforced." [Signed: O.H. Irish, Superintendent, Indian Affairs.]

Nine months after the Uinta River Valley Reservation was confirmed by Congress on May 5, 1864, the Act of February 23, 1865 (13 Stat. 432), was initiated: An Act to "Extinguish the Indian Title to Lands in the Territory of Utah Suitable for Agriculture and Mineral Purposes" which gave rise to the unratified "Spanish Fork Treaty." It was enacted the year after ratification of the reservation and directs the President with the advice and consent of the Senate to enter treaties deemed just to the Indians, provided the Indians surrendered possessory right to all agriculture and mineral lands in the territory except as to agricultural and mineral lands on reservations by such treaties.

On 23 February 1865, Congress passed "an act to extinguish the Indian title to the lands in the Territory of Utah suitable for agriculture and mineral purposes," and on 28 March, Commissioner Dole communicated to Superintendent Irish to proceed with treaty making with the Indian tribes in Utah.[64]

---

64 William P. Dole to O.H. Irish, 28 March, 1865 Utah Superintendent Report No. 29.

The Superintendent and associates met with the invited chiefs on 6 June for preliminary talks and reading of the treaty. (The following proceedings are from the original minutes preserved in the unratified treaties file, Spanish Fork Treaty, 1865, National Archives)

The preamble stated:

Articles of Agreement and Convention made and concluded at Spanish Fork Indian Farm, in the Territory of Utah, this eighth day of June, eighteen hundred and sixty-five by O.H. Irish, Superintendent of Indian Affairs for Said Territory Comm., on the part of the U.S. and the undersigned chiefs, ...on behalf of said Indians and duly authorized by them. At a council of the Utah Indians, held at Spanish Fork Indian Reservation, commencing on the seventh of June 1865 at so which the said Indians were represented by the following chiefs:

Sow-e-ett (Nearly Starved) – Chief Yampah Utahs
Kanosh (Man of White Hair) – Chief Pah-Vants
Tabby (The Sun) – Chief Yampah Utahs
To-quo-ne (Black Mountain Lion) – Chief Yampah
Sow-ok-soo-bet (Arrow Feather) – Chief San Pitch Utahs
An-kar-tew-its (Red Boy) – Chief Timpa-nogs Utahs
Kibets (Mountain) – Chief Spanish Fork Utahs
Am-oosh – Chief Cum-um-bahs
An-kar-an-keg (Red Rifle) – Sub-Chief Pah-Vants
Namp-peades (Foot Mother) – Sub-Chief Timpa-nogs Utahs
Pam-sook (Otter) – Sub-Chief Utahs
Pean-up (Big Foot) – Sub-Chief Pah-Vants
Eah-gand (Shot to Pieces) – Sub-Chief Pah-Vants
Nar-i-ent (Powerful) – Sub-Chief Pah-Vants
Quo-o-gand (Bear) – Sub-Chief Utahs
San Pitch (Bull Rush) – Chief Utahs

The treaty would require the Indians to cede their mineral and agricultural lands in the Salt Lake Valley, and Ashley Valley on the Uinta Valley Reservation. The Indians did not want to give up their lands, the federal records state the following:

"If the talk is for us to trade the land to get the presents, I do not want any blankets or any clothing. I would rather go without than to give up my title to the land I occupy."

Chief San Pitch, Utah Shoshone1865 Spanish Fork minutes, National Archives *"The hearts of the Indians are full; they want to think, wait until tomorrow; let us go back to our lodges and talk and smoke over what has been said today. The Indians are not ready now to give up the land; they never thought of such a thing."* Chief Tabby-To-Kwanah, Utah Shoshone 1865 Spanish Fork minutes, National Archives The Spanish Fork Treaty had reached the Senate on 6 March 1866, where it was referred to the committee on Indian Affairs. Three years later, in February 1869, Senator James Harlan, chairman of that committee, submitted it to O.H. Browning, Secretary of the Interior, with an inquiry as to whether he would recommend ratification.

The Secretary referred Harlan's inquiry to Commissioner of Indian Affairs A.G. Taylor, who replied on 18 February 1869: *The ratification of the treaty with the Utah Tribes has been repeatedly urged by this office, as under its provisions, measures could be adopted for the concentration of the Indians of the Territory upon the ample reservation set apart for their use and occupancy, and the necessary means afforded for their support and improvement. It is possible that a better treaty can be made under present circumstances and relations of these Indians, and I suggest that it would be as well, perhaps, that the Senate, do not* *advise the ratification of the pending treaty – in which event, I would recommend that early steps be taken to negotiate a new one.*[65]

On 11 March 1869, Senator Harlan reported to the Senate. The result was the adoption of a resolution "that the Senate does not advise and consent to the ratification of said treaties." The resolution was forwarded to the President. Only to be returned to the Commissioner's office and buried in the unratified treaty files now located in the National Archives.

By this authority, the headmen and chiefs of the Uinta Shoshone Bands of the Uinta River Valley Reservation consisting of 'Yutas', Uinta-Ats, Yampa, Pah-Vant, San-Pitch, Timpanogos, Pi-ede, Seuvarit, and Cum-mum-bah bands were called to attend a meeting at the Spanish Fork Indian Farm located at the mouth of Provo Canyon; entrance to the Salt Lake Valley, and there on the 8th day of June 1865, they met with Indian Affairs Superintendent O.H. Irish, Commissioner, on the part of the United States, former Governor Brigham Young, and others to negotiate an agreement with said Uinta Valley Shoshone Indians.

As reported in the 1865 Spanish Fork minutes, Chief Tabby-To-Qwanah of the Utah Shoshone stated: *"I love all of you and do not want to see blood shed on the land. I want you to send a good father to Uinta; one that won't quarrel with us, I will go there. I love that country."*

Commonly called the Spanish Fork Treaty, it provided: "Except" for the Uinta River Valley Reservation, the Indians to cede all claims to land in parts of the present states of Utah, Nevada, Arizona, and Colorado an area of approximately 55-million acres of land in exchange for government services and products. Not only

---

65 Record Group 48 – Letters received, Secretary of the Interior. File January to April 1869 – Box 23, National Archives.

Shoshone 'Yutas' but Paiute and Gosiute representatives from southern Utah agreed to this treaty, which in effect was a ratification by the Indians of President Lincoln's Allodial Land Grant creation of the Uinta Valley Indian Reservation in 1861. But only the Uinta Valley Shoshone bands of 'Yutas' seem to have been affected by its provisions, for the Gosiutes settled in Deep Creek and Skull Valley sectors of Tooele County in western Utah, and the Paiutes settled in other western Utah counties, including Juab and Beaver Counties. The Uinta Valley Shoshone Indians, however, soon settled on the said reservation where they were relatively undisturbed until 1880.[66]

The Deseret News (Salt Lake City)
14 JUNE 1865

On Towards Payson: Just outside of Spanish Fork an escort met the President, which passing through the city, headed toward the Indian Reservation Farm. A few minutes brought us into the middle of the lodges and wick-i-ups of the Indians, which were erected on either side of the road, and an astonishing amount of "how" and hand shaking was got through with in a short time. Driving on to the farmhouse a halt was made until some of the chiefs came up, when a short "talk" ensued. The movements of a body of military, proceeding to assist in making the new mail-road, created considerable alarm among them, but on President Young and Colonel Irish assuring them that the military were not coming to the council and did not mean to attack them, they agreed to assemble next morning at ten o'clock for business. The party then proceeded to Payson, where they remained over-night, except Colonel Irish, who returned to the farm to expedite the matter of which he was Commissioner. Meeting With the Indians: Wednesday morning a little

---

66 (Executive Journal, Vol. 17, 1869-71) (Larson, Gustive O. (1974) "Uintah Dream: The Ute Treaty – Spanish Fork, 1865," BYU Studies Quarterly: Vol. 14: Iss.3, Article.

before ten, the President and company drove down to the farm, where under a temporary bowery the Indians were to meet Commissioner Irish, to have the treaty talked over. On the part of the Indians, Sow-e-ette, Kan-osh, Tabby-To-Qwana, Sanpitch, and eleven other chiefs of lesser note, with a large crowd of Indians. The Talk: Colonel Irish called attention to some good acts performed by a few and bestowed presents upon them. He then read an abstract of the treaty, which is quite literal in its provisions, and talked plainly, straight forward and sensibly to them. Kan-osh led off on the part of the Indians. He was a boy, but Sow-e-ette was an old man and could speak; he couldn't, yet he kept on trying and made quite a speech before he got through; Colonel Irish talked with one tongue, but others had talked with two; they had lied to the Indians; would Colonel Irish always talk one way?

They did not want to sell their lands and go away; they wanted to live round the graves of their fathers. San-pitch followed him, and spoke rather bitterly, manifesting a strong desire to exert his influence against the treaty. President Young then talked to them, recalled his counsel and advice to them in the past, assured them he was still their friend, and advised them to sign the treaty and accept the provisions guaranteed in it for their benefit. The effect of his advice manifested itself in a few moments, most of the chiefs being strongly inclined to act upon it at the time, but Tabby counseled waiting a little to calm their minds, so that they might act without any excitement of feeling. The "pow-wow" was consequently adjourned till the next morning. Yours, Respectfully, E. L. Sloan

Although the treaty just described was never ratified by Congress, various individual Indians, and groups of Utahs from time to time after 1865, moved into the Uinta River Valley. An Indian Agency was established there, and the area became known as the

Uinta Indian Reservation. The Shoshone bands of Utahs migrated into the reservation, as well as those already there before the reservation was established, and their descendants, became and have since been known as the Uinta Indians.

The United States Government never entered into a treaty with the Uinta Valley Shoshone. Their original reservation boundaries, "from mountain top to mountain top" comprising the entire Uinta Basin are still intact. The Uinta River Valley Basin Reservation was set apart for the Utah Indians, separate from the public domain by Executive Order 38-1 issued by President Abraham Lincoln in 1861. It was confirmed by the Senate on May 5, 1864 (13 Stat. 63), and the land was settled by various bands and family clans of Shoshone-Yuta Indians, some fleeing from the white settlers in the Salt Lake Valley of the Great Basin in Western Utah. Eventually these Shoshone bands of Utahs amalgamated in the Uinta Valley Basin as a single Tribe of Uinta Valley Shoshone Indians or "Uinta Band" whose ancestors had historically occupied the Great Basin, Salt Lake Valley, and the Uinta Valley Basin in Utah Territory from time immemorial. The early bands called themselves Ne-we (meaning people); others called them "Yutas" as documented by the various Spanish explorers, Indian Agents and in Federal Government documents. The Utah Territory was named after them and eventually when Utah was approved for statehood, the name was kept. Keeping the Uinta Valley Shoshone legacy alive throughout history despite the mass revision of history.

The Shoshone people continue to have aboriginal rights in the Salt Lake Valley and allodial ownership in the Ashley Valley. They have not ceded their lands through agreement or ratified treaty, nor have the Uinta band of Shoshone Utahs been paid for these lands.

The taking was a theft that was not in accordance with federal law for Native Americans.[67]

The Deseret News (Salt Lake City)
26 APRIL 1866

Brothers David H. Cannon and James Andrus reported that San-pitch and four other Indians, who lately escaped from custody in Sanpete Valley, were killed 16th inst., on the mountains east of Nephi, between Sanpete and Juab Valleys. San-pitch and the few with him were a part of those renegade Indians who have been assisting Black Hawk and his renegades in their depredations in Sevier, Sanpete, and Thistle Valleys.

Citizenship – After the American Civil War, the Civil Rights Act of 1866 states, "that all persons born in the United States, and not subject to any foreign power, excluding Indians not taxed, are hereby declared to be citizens of the United States". This was affirmed by the ratification of the Fourteenth Amendment. But the concept of Native Americans as U.S. citizens fell out of favor among politicians at the time. Senator Jacob Howard of Michigan commented, "I am not yet prepared to pass a sweeping act of naturalization by which all the Indian savages, wild or tame, belonging to a tribal relation, are to become my fellow- citizens and go to the polls and vote with me".[68]

In a Senate floor debate regarding the Fourteenth Amendment, James Rood Doolittle of Wisconsin stated, *"all those wild Indians to be citizens of the United States, the Great Republic of the world, whose*

---

67 United States Federal court of Claims No. 47569 Uintah and White Rivers Bands v. United States, 152 F. Supp. 953 (Fed. Cl. Decided Oct 9, 1957.) It was not explained to the Indians that the treaty required ratification by the Senate, and it was formally rejected by the United States Senate on March 11, 1869.

68 Congressional Globe, 1866

citizenship should be a title as proud as that of king, and whose danger is that you may degrade that citizenship." [69]

Pardon Dodd, a veteran of the Civil War, established the first Uinta Indian Agency at White Rocks, in the Uinta Basin, Utah Territory, located at the base of the Uinta Mountains in the Uinta River Valley Basin, northeastern Utah, after it was set apart as a reservation and was the first Indian Agent thereof. The White Rocks Indian Agency was maintained there until Fort Duchesne was established as a military post. The Agency remained there until 1912 when the fort was abandoned. Along with fellow agency workers Morris Evans and John Blankenship, Dodd kept non-Indians off the reservation. He retired in 1872 and returned to the Uinta Basin as a stockman on February 14, 1873. In violation of the 1865 Presidential Order, Dodd built the first cabin in the Ashley Valley located in the northeast end of the reservation to raise livestock along with Morris Evans, Dick Huffaker and the two former fellow agency workers. These men knew that the Ashley Valley was a part of the Uinta Valley Basin Reservation land grant to the Yuta Indians of Utah Territory in 1861 and about the President's Executive Order for white settlers to vacate the reservation in 1865. This disregard for federal actions and federal laws continue to exhibit itself every day among Utah citizens trespassing in Indian Country

The Deseret News (Salt Lake City, Utah)
22 MAY 1867

Utah Indian Superintendency: We have before us the report of 1866 of Colonel F.H. Head, Superintendent of Indian Affairs for Utah. The

---

69 McCool, Daniel, Susan M. Olson, and Jennifer L. Robinson. Native Vote, Cambridge, England: Cambridge University Press, 2007.

document is an interesting one, and creditable alike to the gentleman's humane feelings and intelligence. The Indian tribes within this superintendency are:

1. *The eastern band of Shoshones and the mixed bands of Bannocks and Shoshones; These bands all recognize Washakee as chief. They number about four thousand five hundred souls.*

2. *The northwestern bands of Shoshones. These Indians number about eighteen hundred. Pocatello, Black Beard, and San Pitz are the principal chiefs.*

3. *The western Shoshones. These Indians number about two thousand.*

4. *The Goships or Gosha0Utahs. These Indians number about one thousand.*

5. *The Weber Shoshone or Cum-umbahs. These Indians number about six hundred.*

6. *The Utahs. These Indians are now principally consolidated into two bands, one under the control of Tabby, who has succeeded to the chieftainship made virtually vacant by the old age and infirmity of Sow-i-et. This band is composed of the Tim-pa-nogs, the Uintas, and the San-Pitches, and number about four thousand. The other Utahs are known as Pah-Vants, and are controlled by Kanosh, and number about fifteen hundred.*

7. *The Pah-Edes. These Indians number about six hundred. Their principal chief is Tut-sey-gub-bets.*

8. *The Pah-Utes. These Indians number about six hundred.*

The Deseret News (Salt Lake City)
28 AUGUST 1867

Black Hawk – We had the pleasure of meeting Superintendent Head on Wednesday evening, who had arrived from Uinta Reservation, where he had met and had talked with the notorious Black Hawk, who came there with his family, unattended by his warriors. Black Hawk said he has 28 lodges under his sole control; and that he was assisted by 5 Elk Mountain chiefs, who have each 10 or 12 lodges with them. These Indians are scattered along the settlements, he travels, from the north of Sanpete County to the southern settlements, watching opportunities to make raids. He expressed a desire for peace; said he could control and would be answerable for his band; and believed he could get the others with him, as they all looked to him as the head chief. He would try and get them all together at some point, perhaps at Uinta, to have a talk with Colonel Head; but it would take some time to do this, as they are so scattered. As I am earnest of his sincerity, he stated that he had made a covenant, when he commenced to fight, that he would not have his hair cut, and he had talked strong of Tabby and Kan-osh whose had theirs cut like white men; but now that he was going to have peace, he wished to have it cut, and requested the Superintendent to shorten his locks for him, which was done after finding that he was anxious to have it so. The savage was saucy at the opening of the interview, but finally toned down, and talked reasonable before they got through.

The Deseret News (Salt Lake City)
26 AUGUST 1868

Indian Treaty – Colonel F.H. Head, Superintendent of Indian Affairs, and Major Dimick B Huntingdon, Indian Interpreter, returned to the city yesterday afternoon from Strawberry Valley, Uinta, where a "big talk" had been held on Wednesday with the Indians, and a treaty concluded with those who have been continuing depredatory visits to our settlements in Sanpete. Black Hawk was present, but it is claimed that he has faithfully observed the treaty made last year and has not been engaged in any raid on the whites since. Those with whom the "talk" was principally held, and who signed the treaty, were Aug-a-vor-um, Tam-a ritz and Sow-ah-point, chiefs of the Shub-er-ech Indians. The first named is the principal chief and is young and feminine looking. The second has been the prime mover in several of the raids made on our settlements, and in the murder of whites, which have been before time accredited to Black Hawk. He was the chief who was riding the white horse in one of the battles with the Indians, who was severely wounded, and was supposed to be Black Hawk, at the time it was reported that Black Hawk was killed. He was of the party who murdered Major Vance and Sergeant Houtz and was at other places where whites were killed. The "talk" with these chiefs was a lengthy one, occupying nearly all day; and while it was progressing the lodge was surrounded by warriors and squaws waiting for the result. Finally, they concluded to bury the hatchet, and be at peace with the whites, and a treaty was concluded, which Major Huntingdon believes they will observe; but our brethren in the settlements who are exposed to their incursions will do well to remember that "eternal vigilance is the price of safety," and keep themselves ever ready to guard their lives, their families and property from Indian attacks.

The Deseret News (Salt Lake City, Utah)
16 DECEMBER 1868

Springtown, Dec. 4, 1868: On the 1st of November last we were visited by the Indians Tah-be-u-ner, Un-gitz-rib and Tah-rue-good of the

Utah tribe, who wished to know our feelings in relation to peace. They came well recommended by the interpreter at the Uinta reservation and were said to be men of influence. They said they wanted a "big talk" and to make a "big peace." In the eye of the law, we did not consider ourselves authorized to treat with them, this being a matter over which the Government exercises exclusive jurisdiction; but on second thought, we concluded that we would do something, as it appeared to us a very opportune time to establish a permanent understanding with them, and as there were no Government officers present, we thought there could be no harm in doing good of ourselves, and that the Government would not be jealous at our action in the case. They wanted pay for the killing of Sanpitch and the men that were with him, and they wanted a large pay in the shape of horses, beef-cattle, blankets, guns, ammunition, flour, shirts, tobacco, and different articles of clothing. On the 3d of November our Bishops all came together and we told them from that we felt very differently towards them from what we should, if we had begun the war; but the war was begun by them; that they had stolen our horses, cattle and had killed our men, women, and children. They did not like to admit that they had begun the war; but, after a little conversation, and the introduction of testimony, they did admit it. We told them we did not have anything to give them for the killing of Sanpitch and his men; that they were in prison, and if they had remained there quietly, they would no doubt have been alive and with them to-day; but as they broke out of jail and attempted to escape, they were shot down by the guard, they not being able to capture them without. We told them that we had nothing to give them for the killing of those prisoners; but we told them we would make them a present of something before they left; that we wanted peace, and that we always wanted it, and never wanted war. We told them that they owed us, *more than they could ever pay, consequently, we should ask them for nothing.*

The Deseret News (Salt Lake City, Utah)
2 JUNE 1869

Par-Vants – Mus-so-quibe, An-kar-tah and Scar-up, with twelve of their men and a herd of ponies are in our city on their way to pay a parting visit to Wash-i-kee, of the Snakes, who is in the vicinity of Bridger. The Par-vants want robes, and Wash-i-kee ponies to move his people north into Canada. Having sold his old home to the Government, he now seeks another where there is more game and greater seclusion from wicked whites, who he says have not only debased themselves but have corrupted the Indian women, in consequences of which disease is thinning his band very fast and causing a far greater loss than the blankets and other gifts are worth. The Par-vants had planted quite a breadth of grain at their late home that looked well at the time they left. "Black Hawk" In the City – Major Dymock D. Huntington, Indian Interpreter, informs us that on the evening of Friday last, he had a visit from the notorious Chief "Black Hawk," who has been the prime mover in the Indian disturbances for the last few years in the southern portion of this Territory. "Black Hawk" said he was sent by the Pi-edes, who live on Gunnison's trail and the Spanish Trail, west of the Green River. They want peace and "Black Hawk" said he would have them all, - men, women, and children in Gunnison in one moon, so that the Indian Superintendent, Colonel Head, and he, Dymock, might go and have a talk with them. He says they will not want to talk with them. He says they will not want to come to Gunnison, because they have nothing but horses they have stolen from the "Mormons" to ride on; they would rather meet a distance from the settlement. However, as

"Black Hawk" has kept his promise to keep the peace, given two years ago, it is very likely that he will bring them. The Pi-edes see what presents the Shib-er-ech Indians, living north of Spanish trail and west of Green River, have got by being peaceful, and they are anxious to reap similar benefits themselves. "Black Hawk" says Tab-by-Uner has lately stolen six horses from the vicinity of Payson and taken them East to trade them off; and he thinks more vigilance is necessary in that neighborhood. Repentant Indians – Brother Dimick H. Huntington reached this city from Sanpete on Monday evening and brings with him a good report of the Indians. He met and had a talk with about 120 of them at Fort Ephraim, about noon last Saturday. President Orson Hyde, and Bishops Johnson and Peterson, and a good number of the brethren were present during the pow-wow. "Black Hawk" brought the crowd in, among whom was "Tam-a-rits," a Shib-ar-ech Chief, the one who is known as the rider of the white horse, who has committed most of the murders during the Indian disturbances South and is regarded as being a much worse man than "Black Hawk" himself. Five of the principal men spoke on the occasion, expressing themselves very humbly and penitently over their past bad deeds, and asking what they must do to be saved. "Black Hawk" said that for four years they had had no heart, but now they had got heart, eyes, and ears, and could both see and hear. They agreed to protect the settlers and give them warning when mischief was threatened by marauding Indians and agreed to bring in all Indians, they could who are still marauding and bent on mischief. "Black Hawk" recommended that a telegram be sent to Qunn-ar-row, at Parowan, for him to send out his own sons to bring in the wicked Indians who committed the recent depredations in that neighborhood. During the conservation the Indians wanted to know who was making bad medicine and killing all the rabbits in the valley, as they are dying

off in great numbers. Brother Huntington informed them it was a disease among them.

The Deseret News (Salt Lake City)
30 DECEMBER 1869

Parowan, December 22d, 1869 Dear Brother Cannon: - On the 16th instant, we had a big visit from Black Hawk, his brother Mountain and quite a number, of his band. Black Hawk and Mountain talked to the people in the meeting house in the evening, brother Shelton, from Beaver, being the interpreter. Black Hawk made great declarations of friendship and said he wanted a big peace, a strong peace, and a long peace. The day before his arrival, the Navajos had made a raid on our horses, and a company of men were in pursuit. Black Hawk offered to go and bring the horses back, if we would furnish him and his men fresh horses to ride, but it was not seen fit to accept his generous offer. He told us to catch the Navajos, if we could, when they came to steal, and not kill them, but talk to them and show that we do not desire to shed blood; send them back to their home and friends to tell what was said to them. This he said, "would do far better than killing them." This is very good advice but comes with rather a bad grace from such a quarter. He said that he wished to see the settlements on the Sevier River established again and promised that they should not be disturbed by the Utah's. – Black Hawk's consumptive look, and hollow cough indicate that he cannot last long.

His brother Mountain, a thoughtful and intelligent looking Indian, then addressed the meeting, and said that he had always told the Indians, when they wanted him to join their raids, that he would not go, for he had horses to ride, and when he wanted anything to eat, he could kill deer and rabbits, and always advised the Indians to stay at home. The Indians present testified to the truth of what he said. He told them that they had stolen hundreds of cattle and horses, and they were poorer now than ever, and they always would be poor while they continued to steal. Now they had no chief - they were all under-ground, and they would all die, if they did not do better. He says he does not want to shed the blood of anybody but wants all to live till God wants them to die. This Indian I believe to be no coward, has a great influence among the tribe, and will likely be the chief at Black Hawk's death. The people had to furnish them the usual amount of beef, biscuits, and flour, and they went on their way rejoicing. W.C. McGregor

CHAPTER 16:

1870's

The Deseret News (Salt Lake City, Utah)
25 MAY 1870

*Indians in Town – Tabby, (the sun), and to To-quer-oner, (black fox), with
some of their men came in yesterday on a visit to Colonel Tourtelotte,
Superintendent of Indian Affairs for the Territory. They talk and feel first
rate. They say they are not going to steal, and their men have gone to
the settlements to get tshut-cup, (bread). Thirty lodges, under An-ter-ro-
ve-yea-hoo, have gone to fight the Sioux; and twenty lodges have gone
to Wash-i-kie to trade. They report that the Navajos or Pah-witches,
are a good deal disaffected; but as soon as they, (Tabby and To-quer-
oner), return they say they will send a delegation of their men to invite
the Navajos to come in and trade, stop stealing, and be friends with the
Mormons. They also report that Hawes, a soldier discharged from Bridger,
who was killed last winter, at the junction of the White and Green Rivers,
met his death at the hands of the Elk Mountain Indians.*

The Deseret News (Salt Lake City, Utah)
25 MAY 1870

Indians – We learn from Mr. M.J. Shelton, Government Interpreter for Uinta, is from the Indian reservation, Uinta Valley, that the Tabbywatts, Piemps, and Yampy-Utahs from the White-River country, and the Uinta Utahs, Gosho-Utahs, Snakes, Bannocks, and other northern tribes of Indians are now assembling in the Bannock country, about fifty miles east of the Bear Lake Valley, to engage in their traditional religious rites. Lest the people in that northern country should become alarmed at so many Indians assembling, they wish it understood that they mean peace; and that after getting through with their religious service, they will again disperse. Mr. Shelton will return immediately to the reservation.

The Ogden Junction (Ogden, Utah)
25 JUNE 1870

Indian Camp: On a level bench overlooking the whole valley the red men of the mountains had gathered in from various parts and set up their wickiups. There were the Utahs, Yampah Utahs, Snakes, a few Bannacks, Half-breeds, Mexicans etc., numbering about 1,800. They were peaceable and friendly, had not met for hostile purposes, but to hold council according to general annual custom. Tabby was there – chief of the Utahs, and Jem his brother – a splendidly formed athletic brave, his face painted, and his broad chest covered with beads. Tsi-gwitch-chief of several bands of Shoshones, Tapah-boona-seheeb (Shake a rabbit out of the bush) chief of the Snakes under Washakie, Toqueroner (Black Fox) old Sowiatt's son, Pocotello, Black Hawk, etc. Most of these chiefs came up to the company and shook hands. Tabby did not present himself. Our friend "Dimick" had a talk with him and upbraided him for having stolen horses in his band while none were found among the other tribes. This made Tabby ashamed and a little mad, so he kept out of the way.

The Deseret News (Salt Lake City)
30 SEPTEMBER 1870

Spring Lake Villa September 27th, 1870 Editor Deseret News: Dear Sir – I hasten to tell you that Black Hawk, the Indian desperado, is dead. He has been living here in camp with his brother "Mountain," together with "Joe" and his band for some days. We knew he was sick but did not think of so sudden a demise. This morning, before, sun-up the Indian wail was heard in their camp, and soon was seen one Indian squaw with two horses heavily packed, on their way towards the foot of the mountain. Stopping at a small ravine within sight of our door, they killed one of the horses and proceeded to put away the body of the great Black Hawk. This is the place of his birth. Here he commenced his depredations, and here he came back to die. Showan, a friendly Indian, the head of the camp about here, died at Goshen a few days since, and Queant, another good Indian, lies in camp about to die. Really, our Indian neighbors are fast passing away! Indian "Joe," the present head of the Indians about here, is here, telling me about the death of Black Hawk, and many other things that I cannot so well understand. He wants me to tell Brigham and Brother Hyde not to let the Green River Indians have any powder, for they lie and steal, and they must be watched, or they will take more horses this fall. He wishes the Mormons to know that he died in his camp. Faithfully yours, B.F. Johnson

The Deseret News (Salt Lake City)
27 SEPTEMBER 1870

Black Hawk – We have received the following dispatch per Deseret Telegraph Line: Payson, September 27 – Black Hawk died at the Indian camp, three miles south of here, last night. John Spencer, Interpreter

Indian Appropriations Act of 1871

In 1871 Congress added a rider to the Indian Appropriations Act ending United States recognition of additional Native American tribes or independent nations and prohibiting additional treaties. That hereafter no Indian nation or tribe within the territory of the United States shall be acknowledged or recognized as an independent nation, tribe, or power with whom the United States may contract by treaty: Provided, further, that nothing herein contained shall be construed to invalidate or impair the obligation of any treaty heretofore lawfully made and ratified with any such Indian nation or tribe. The President's power to create Indian Reservations by executive order was amended to require ratification by the Senate after 1871.

The Deseret News (Salt Lake City, Utah)
28 AUGUST 1872

Tabby has always advised the Indians not to steal or kill anybody, but during the last moon there has been some trouble in Sanpete, and Tabby is ashamed of it. Tabby on seeing Superintendent Dodge writing at the table, asked the General if he was writing good. The General said he was. Tabby said when they met at Fairview, he talked to harsh to them and made their hearts cry. If he now feels better towards them all right. They formed a very unfavorable impression of him. When they met at the Reservation and have something to eat and are treated right, they liked it very well, and if the Doctor feels better to them now, all right. "I have not thrown up going to Uinta. Am here on a visit. When did I throw any of you away? When did I steal from you? I have not given up my country. I like it. I always feel well. My heart is good towards all mankind. I consider all mankind are of one flesh and should have feelings alike. Whom have I lied too? When have I hidden anything from you, or deceived any of you? I have not done it. The boys and all have heard the General talk, and they now feel well. I do not lie, and I believe the General talked as I now am talking. I desire that all the Mormons, miners and everybody shall travel these mountains in peace, work and lie down in peace. We do not want any trouble on the roads in or to and around this country. In Sanpete is all the trouble, but no one have been killed in my land at any times. The Indians down there do not have many old men among them, they are all young. As to going to Washington, I do not know what to think about it. We will have to have a meeting about that. Suppose we will go by the iron road. We have some Indians out hunting. I am glad to receive blankets, provisions, etc. given by the government, yet some do not feel well in receiving them, as they think it is for their land. A long time ago the whites came to this country and traded for furs etc. Brigham came and has dealt with them. Indians did not think of killing whites until after the whites killed the Indians. But now the General has talked, and we believe him. He has talked good, and our hearts are one. Want the General to give some of the chiefs a recommend, that they have attended this meeting, and they are good. General Morrow said "With the whites, we say it is good to settle one thing at a time, where we have more than one thing to do. Then we pass that. We want to talk of your grievances, or of sending your Indians to Washington. If you do not conclude about going to Washington now, you can talk it over when you get to the agency. Tabby said they would wait till they got to the agency to talk this over. He asked General Morrow to obtain authority from Washington for them to go to Washington, so if they concluded to go it would be all right. Antero said he felt good and would go to Washington. The General said he wanted Tabby to go. Tabby answered he must stay at home and take care of his men. Waundaroads wanted to go and on the way visit his brother at school in Chester Co., Pennsylvania. General Morrow said he heard the Indians claimed this land and wanted rent for it, that he also heard that a treaty had been made at Spanish Fork, which was not satisfactory, and "you should tell all about it to the Great Father," also heard that Uinta was not a good place for farming. Wanroads said it was. Tabby said that at the Spanish Fork treaty Colonel Irish told them that if they would go to Uinta, he would give them beef, flour, guns, powder, shirts, and everything they needed. "We went over, and I have been on guard ever since, some three or four years, but I have not seen it come yet. You need not take my word for this. There are many here now who heard it, but it was a big lie." The General remarked they would probably find it when they got back. Tabby said, "No, all that Irish said has gone to the grass. We do not want to remember it," and that he would send most of the Indians to camp, and he and some of the others would remain and meet the General in the morning.

The Deseret News (Salt Lake City, Utah)
20 AUGUST 1872

Spanish Fork – This morning General Morrow and command arrived at Springville. Arrangements were made for a conference with the Indians. They traveled up the Spanish Fork canyon four miles, where the Indians had gathered. The company started, and before they got out of Springville met Wanderodes and Jim Uinta, which were on the way to see the General, with whom they had a short interview, in which the General informed them that he wanted peace and wished the Indians to return to the reservation; he wanted them to come and see him at any point they might select outside the canyon; that he knew many of them, having formed their acquaintance, four or five years ago, at Fort Bridger; told them they need not be afraid to come and see him and talk, and lay all their grievances before him-all abuses, if any, practiced upon them by the agents sent among them, if they (the agents) had stolen their rations or kicked their squaws out of doors, he wished them to tell him of it, and not to hide anything and that he would be equally frank with them; and that he would have them feasted during such time as the meeting lasted; and when it was over, if they did not arrange in regard to future friendly relations, that there should be no advantage taken of their being out of the canyon, but they should have the privilege of returning to where they came from. He also wished them to select a delegation to go to Washington and communicate to the Great Father all the wrongs they had to complain of, also their wishes and desires. After this talk, which was to Wanrodes to carry to Tabby, the two Indians joined President Smoot and party and proceeded to the canyon. Arrived at the place appointed, they found Tabby, Douglas, Antero, and some thirty of forty other Indians, all looking cheerful - not a frown from anyone. Wanroads had preceded us a little and told them the sayings of General Morrow, but it was all reiterated by President Smoot and interpreted by L.S. Woods. Wanrodes, the Indian, said it was all right, all good. Tabby said he had the same peace talk now that he always had, that he knew General Morrow a little and would meet him at Springville tomorrow. Wanrodes expresses but little confidence in getting peace with the Seuv-a-rits. The Indians reported as such that came in yesterday, were not, but some Indians from east of Green River.

The Deseret News (Salt Lake City, Utah)
19 SEPTEMBER 1872

The Guilty Indians – On very good authority we are enabled to state that the Indians who have been doing the stealing lately in Springtown, Spanish Fork and Thistle Valley, are from the Reservation, and that the names of the ringleaders are Tangigand, Antero's son-in-law, Pansook, Tangigand sub, or right-hand man in the operations, Jake, Arapene's son, and Wanrodes, the entire band including some six or seven others. Wanrodes stole six or seven head of horses lately from Spanish Fork; and Tangigand, Pansook, Jake and their party recently stole 50 horses from the three places first named. We are also informed that all the stealing that has been done in Sanpete has been done by Indians from the Reservation. Nobody in the settlements desires that any, but guilty Indians should be punished, and as proof of their criminality can now, we are assured, be obtained, we hope to hear of their speedy arrest by those whose business it is, for if they are secured, difficulties will most likely cease, but until then there is little probability of such a desirable result.

The Utah Mining Journal (Salt Lake City)
9 OCTOBER 1872

The Indian Delegation, which will probably go to Washington in ten or twelve days are Antero, Wanrodes, Tabiona, Snap-no-kin and Kanosh. Dr. Dodge, special Indian Agent will accompany them with an interpreter. They will leave as soon as arrangements are perfected with the Indian Department. It is hoped this visit will have a beneficial result in opening the eyes of the savages to the power and numbers of the whites in the land. To-day the "noble savages" are riding about town clad in purple and calico, a dignified and magnificent as any chiefs. They are living sumptuously at Camp Douglas, and dispatch their full rations like men and brothers, and pine not, nor are they cast down and dejected. Lo! Is an institution better observed in Camp Douglas and the highways of a city than in his native wilds, where his tendency to "raise hair" is more readily indulged in.

The Deseret News (Salt Lake City, Utah)
23 OCTOBER 1872

Indian Delegation – A delegation of Indians, accompanied by Dr. Dodge, Indian Agent, and Mr. George Bean, of Provo, the latter in the capacity of interpreter, left for Washington this morning, for the purpose of laying their grievances before President Grant. The Indians composing the delegation are Wanrodes, Antero, Tabiona and Kanosh.

By 1869 Congress declared they had no intention of ratifying the Spanish Fork Treaty. Even after eight years had passed since the treaty was signed, the leadership of the Utahs came to Salt Lake City to discuss the terms that they had agreed to. It appears that no one had explained to them that it had not been ratified and was not binding on either party. By this time, all the Shoshone bands of Utahs had moved to the Uinta Valley Reservation.[70]

---

70 Report of Special Commissioners J.W. Powell and G.W. Ingalls Washington, D.C., December 18, 1873

The Ogden Junction (Ogden, Utah)
15 OCTOBER 1873

Tabby, head chief of the Utahs, Wanrodes, Mountain, Pete, Tabbi-oo-na, Pe-Ke-ats and Richard Koomas are at Salt Lake on business connected with the unconfirmed treaty of Spanish Fork. The Indians held to its terms, but the Government does not recognize it.

The Deseret News (Salt Lake City, Utah)
10 OCTOBER 1873

Indian Chiefs – The Indian Chiefs, Tabiona, Wanrodes and Tabby, were being conducted around the city by Interpreter D.B. Huntington today. Tabby is failing very much, being nearly blind. Tabiona is rather a fine, pleasant looking, broad-chested old fellow, and is very suave and affable in his manner. They are on visit here, from the Uinta Reservation. They propose starting back for the latter place tomorrow.

The Deseret News (Salt Lake City, Utah)
15 OCTOBER 1873

Territorial Dispatches – Per Deseret Telegraph Line: Spanish Fork – Tabby, Chief of the Utahs, with several his sub-chiefs, are here from the reservation, looking and feeling well. They propose visiting Salt Lake City in a few days and then returning to the reserve at Uinta.

The Ogden Junction (Ogden, Utah)
15 OCTOBER 1873

Tabby, head chief of the Utahs, Wan-rodes, Mountain, Pete, Tabbi-oo-na, Pe-Ke-ats and Richard Koomas, are at Salt Lake on business connected with the unconfirmed treaty of Spanish Fork. The Indians are held to its terms, but the Government does not recognize it. Richard is an educated Indian, having been to Lincoln University, in Pennsylvania, and he is much interested in the affairs of his tribe. He will doubtless make a mark in their history.

"The Indians of Utah and Nevada, known as Shoshones by the whites, are known by very different names by the Indians. "The two tribes mentioned, Pah-vants and Seuv-a-rits, speak the same language, and are intermarried with the Indians on the Uinta Reservation, and should be taken there. "The Go-si Utes (Goshutes) speak a language more nearly like that of the Indians at Fort Hall, but they are intermarried and affiliate with the Indians at the Uintah reservation, and it is believed they would prefer to go there also. "Under these circumstances, your commissioners did not deem that it would be wise to remove any of the Indians at present, and they submit this statement of the condition of affairs for your consideration. Having in view the ultimate removal of all the foregoing Indians to reservations already established, the following recommendations are made: "First. That the Pah-vants and Seuv-a-rits be visited and informed that the Government of the United States has decided that they shall make their homes on the Uinta reservation, and that hereafter no goods will be issued to them at any other place. "Second. That the tribes of Pai-Utes shall be visited and, if possible, several chiefs and principal men be induced, to visit the Uintah reservation with a view to their final settlement at that place. Removal with favor, it should then make a thorough examination into the condition of affairs on the Muddy Reservation and report the results to the Department. "The agent for that reservation immediately commence work and prepare to raise a crop the coming year to such an extent. as the appropriation and circumstances on the reservation will permit. In the meantime, two or three reliable men should be employed by the commission.[71]

During the summer of 1877, John Hiatt, passed through Ashley Valley located in the eastern most part of the Uinta Valley Reservation, and was favorably impressed with it. Upon arrival at Huntsville, he told Thomas Bingham Sr. who wanted to see for himself. Being satisfied that the Country was a good one, he reported his findings to President John Taylor of the L.D.S. (Mormon) Church, who endorsed the move to colonize the Ashley Valley area of the Uinta Valley Reservation. In addition to those who came on their own initiative, several were called by the church to settle in the Ashley Valley that sixteen (16) years earlier the Mormon leader Brigham Young had rejected for his settlers and did not object, at that time in 1861, to the creation of said reservation, saying the area was only fit for nomadic Indians and to hold the rest of the world together.

Previous Indian Agent, Pardon Dodd and company had been trespassing in the Ashley Valley for four years by this time. J.J. Critchlow replaced Pardon Dodd as superintendent. Critchlow's tenure as Agent was from 1872 to 1883, but he did not enforce the reservation boundaries that would have kept white people and fellow ex-agent Dodd, employees Evans and Blankenship and the Mormon Church out of the Ashley Valley, who were knowingly violating the executive order of 1861.

Utah's Indian tribes went into a steady and irreversible decline after 1847, that they never recovered from. They endured decades of white power, disease, and murder. Only to realize it was not enough, the white settlers wanted more and would plan and scheme to genocide the Uinta Valley Shoshone and take all they had.

---

71 J. W. Powell, G. W. Ingalls, U.S. Special Commission 1874

To Be Continued.

Dora Van is the Chairwoman of the Uinta Valley Shoshone Tribe. Through her leadership, the people, have banded together and remained viable, she resides on the Uinta Valley Reservation (aka Uinta & Ouray Agency) in Utah.

Tressa Jordan is the Vice-Chairwoman of the Uinta Valley Shoshone Tribe. Without her long hours of research, this book would not be possible, she resides on the Uinta Valley Reservation (aka Uinta & Ouray Agency) in Utah.

John Torres has been a researcher for the Uinta Valley Shoshone Tribe for many years. His contribution and assistance in researching Spanish, Mexican and U.S. Military documents has been invaluable.